GETTING BERGSON STRAIGHT

The Contributions of Intuition to the Sciences

Pete A. Y. Gunter

University of North Texas

Series in Philosophy

VERNON PRESS

In the Americas:	*In the rest of the world:*
Vernon Press	Vernon Press
1000 N West Street, Suite 1200,	C/Sancti Espiritu 17,
Wilmington, Delaware 19801	Malaga, 29006
United States	Spain

Series in Philosophy

Library of Congress Control Number: 2022946092

ISBN: 978-1-64889-737-5

Also available: 978-1-64889-503-6 [Hardback]; 978-1-64889-633-0 [PDF, E-Book]

Cover design by Vernon Press.
Cover image: (top) courtesy of Department of Histology, Jagiellonian University Medical College; (bottom) image by Gerd Altmann from Pixabay.

Table of Contents

Acknowledgments

I would like to thank Keith "Maggie" Brown and Christopher Peterson for their typing, for their persistence, and for their insightful reflections on this book. I would also like to thank my daughter, Sheila D. Gunter, for her editorial help, without which this study would be far less intelligible than it is.

Foreword

Randall E. Auxier

Southern Illinois University Carbondale

The book you are reading is the result of more than a half century of learning and achievement in the philosophy of science. In particular, this book attempts to situate the philosophy of Henri Bergson in light of our latest science. It shows that Bergson's key ideas anticipated positions we now need to adopt widely in order to accommodate, philosophically, the trends and discoveries of today's science. The main reason to involve Bergson in this effort is not to give credit where it is due (although that should be done), but rather, Bergson still has many ideas that will lead us in the right direction in the future. Bergson's contribution to our self-understanding is only now becoming clear.

I think I can safely let the book speak for itself in terms of the detail, since it is clear, concise, and accessible to non-specialists in both the philosophy of science and the thought of Bergson. Bergson's philosophy is extremely difficult to understand, even though it seems deceptively straight-forward when one begins reading. Really plumbing the depths of the ideas and their relations is, however, a task that requires years of work. Obviously Pete Gunter put in those years and here presents us with the summary results, at least as regards the general outlines of the Bergsonian philosophy.

One reason this project is necessary is that Bergson is enjoying a long delayed re-consideration. His thought has never wholly disappeared, since many important philosophers, from Whitehead and Merleau-Ponty, through Bachelard, Deleuze, up to the present have made good use of Bergson's ideas in developing our awareness of time. Also the occasional scientist, notably Ilya Prigogine, would bring Bergson back into the conversation. The descent of Bergson's thought always remained significant, but perhaps not as significant as it should have been. Einstein's allies and minions did a hatchet-job on Bergson as a philosopher of science, as documented by Jimena Canales in the 2015 book, *The Physicist and the Philosopher*. Canales' investigation shows that Einstein's intent was to replace philosophy with physics, and one can say he largely succeeded.

Part of the reason that Bergson is on the rise again is that the philosophical weaknesses of Einstein's picture of the universe have finally caught up to the fantasies of the physicists. The need to demand that our experience of time is not real, in the sense that it is not an important or reliable source for knowledge of the physical universe, never sat well with most of the philosophers. The public did not appreciate the depth of this claim, thinking they could have their experience of time and their General Relativity too. Philosophers of science knew better, and split into camps depending upon how objectionable they found the construct of spacetime. If we follow Canales' account, we can see that if Henri Poincare had lived another ten years, the history of 20th century science would be very different. We would not have given Einstein's new block universe a hundred years of ascendency.

But now Bergson's re-assessment has been coming mainly from Continental philosophers who are impressed by certain limited aspects of Bergson's ideas. Bergson was talented at phenomenological descriptions of our experience, even though he was not a defender of phenomenology. Yet, it is tempting to draw on some of his deeper insights about experienced time and ignore the radically empirical framework, which is a philosophy of science, within which these descriptions emerge. That is the situation this book corrects. As Bergson re-emerges and Einstein's universe passes into a very real past, Gunter believes, and rightly, that we must include the work with and on science to get Bergson straight. Thus, Gunter corrects misperceptions and misreadings that have persisted for decades while also re-balancing current readings that are too one-sided.

I have said something, then, about the book, and will let it speak for itself. But I want to say something about the author, since, in a way, this is a culminating effort regarding his extensive work on Bergson. I also want to situate the work on Bergson in the larger context of Gunter's overall work. In the more than 30 years I have known Pete Gunter, I have had the privilege of learning a good deal about what you might call "the man behind the philosopher." Among the most personable of Texans, the man is not only easy to get to know, he's difficult to resist. Pete seems to know everyone and everyone seems to know Pete (so, pardon my familiar way, but I can't bring myself to call the man "Gunter" in the part that follows.) I mean this in the best way, but Pete is a born storyteller, and I don't think the connection between that gift and his philosophical pursuits is incidental. It's just a little hard to puzzle out.

The more one looks at Gunter's life and achievements, the more evident the core of his interests –he needs Bergson, time, physics, and biology to serve a broader concern: nature. The Renaissance man –philosopher, environmentalist, composer, songwriter, novelist, historian, genealogist, humanitarian—begins to come into focus only when you realize that Pete Gunter is a fellow *out for a good time*. But that doesn't mean just what it sounds like. The emphasis must be on the word "time." A "good time" is the best a finite person can hope to achieve in life, or if not wholly good, at least something interesting to mitigate the repetition. To have time is to live an imperative to use it and endure it well. We have minds only to facilitate action, Bergson says, and Pete has taken it as an imperative.

These creative projects, in art, literature, and even political organizing, bear an essential relation to his philosophical thinking, and his most significant endeavor: his environmentalism. Whether we like it or not, philosophy is autobiographical and to deny this violates the first principle of philosophy – that its aim is self-knowledge. So even though the connections among these far-flung contributions may seem vague, they are not only real but also have a determining influence of what we think and how we say it.

The reason for the connection is simple: we do not come to know ourselves apart from what we *do*, our actions (and thinking is an activity, after all). If we wish to know what we *can* do, our actions must break creative ground (at least for us, as individual actors). We constantly do things we haven't done before, and our way of adapting our own bodies to needed movements that negotiate the world end up navigating a *terra incognita* for each of us. Whether you realize it or not, there is a way *you* tie your shoes, brush your teeth, even button your shirt, and it's yours alone. Your acts, *not* some category of acts, but *your* individual acts, over time, become generalized, refined, fluid, and thus, your body *becomes* a reservoir for a general field of action that you may or may not enact. That field of possible acts accompanies you everywhere you go as a generalized body. I summarize here a view explained by Bergson in *Creative Evolution*, of course.

For example, you might be able to play the guitar, as Pete can; or you might be able to imitate a citizen of France or Germany who speaks English with an accent, as Pete can; or perhaps you can write funny songs, as Pete can. The same can be said for anything else you have learned to do by repeated action and refinement over time. And you *can* do these things even when you aren't actually *doing* them. It is a generalized capacity or power that your body *is*. Generalization thus exists in the field of actions, both possible and actual, in the sense that the possible actions exist as paths of movement even when not followed.

For this reason, and for other reasons, if you want to know whether you can become good at writing, for example, you have to write, to enact it –you have to *care* about it, choose it over and over. It's something we do with our bodies, and there is a good deal of mediation between inspiration, idea, act, and product. To create a more or less smooth set of transitions between the impulse to write and having written something "good," then, is an effort involving many exercises and enactments. To have a "talent" for such a thing means that one is able to refine and smooth the path.

In what follows, I want to talk about that process of creation, as Bergson understands it, and bring his view to bear on the creative work of Pete Gunter, both as a philosopher and as an interpreter of Bergson. Anyone who has ever known Pete Gunter, even if only briefly, knows that he tells stories. His stories are usually historical, whether casual recollections, or observations about human oddities, foibles, and failings, or ones that start out with "did you know that . . ." followed by some remarkable tidbit of fact. If he tells you a story in conversation, it usually ends with a question and a shake of the head, a sort of "can you believe that?" and truth-is-stranger-than-fiction sigh. He writes like he talks, and in spite of what many people may believe, that isn't easy to do. It takes practice. The style is straight, easy, sometimes wry.

His novels, for instance, are excavations of his family's past, and always with the sense that there is something inescapable about one's family line. It isn't about fate, or destiny; it's about the *active presence* of the past, but also about the *weight* of the past. Bergson holds that nothing of the past is lost in the present and all of the past is *actively* present, and Pete's writing addresses and claims that point of view. In the long run, the weight becomes too much to bear and vitality becomes too diffused to bring about meaningful change. But as he writes in a song, "the second law of thermodynamics is a Heraclitean law." (Yes, Pete wrote a folk song about entropy.)

Pete's novel, *River in Dry Grass*, ends with the protagonist coming to a momentous decision: for him to let the past be buried and to disappear. In short, he decides to defy, if he can, Bergson's principle about the full and active presence of the past. If the past can't be undone, and it cannot, then why not at least put it to sleep? This is the protagonist's choice, and the reasons for it, insofar as there are any, don't add up and never will and never can. Justice cannot really be served when everyone deserves worse than he or she is getting, so mercy is a new secular universalism. There are no fallen angels begging for redemption, just earthly exiles seeking resident amnesty. To understand, really, what would lead someone to devote so much effort to interpreting a philosopher like Bergson, it helps to see something of the "theology" behind it.

Philosophy and Fiction

The perennial question that arises when one considers a philosopher who writes fiction is "what's the connection, if there is one?" Of course, there have been many philosophers who were truly great writers, and Henri Bergson was certainly among the best –they gave him the Nobel Prize for literature, but philosophy is all he wrote (I doubt that could happen in our day). On the other hand, philosophical imagination usually isn't dominated by narrative structure. The order we find in philosophers tends to me more architectonic. Yet, I encourage readers to approach this book as a sort of story. Imagine that you are getting a complex fireside story by an uncle, somewhat eccentric, whom you have known your whole life. This book is written in formal style, so you will need to insert, occasionally, "and would you believe . . ." and with an occasional, "now, you won't know about this, but . . . ." when the connecting tissue of the story is added, I think you will see that you don't want to nod off until this one is over.

I have had the opportunity to read quite a lot of Pete's academic work, and sometimes it seems to me that I'm dealing with two completely different writers, if I compare it to the non-academic stuff. But Pete has been one of my principal teachers in the area of Bergson studies, and so I can hear that connecting tissue when I read it. He puts a good bit of that in when he delivers an academic paper. It helps with understanding, then, to imagine the accent and the uncle, and the fireside. You should try it.

Pete Gunter is well known in the philosophy profession, and beyond it, as a songwriter. The legend of his songs passes from cohort to cohort among professional philosophers and thus, his recording, *Chicken Fried Escargot* has become as much pirated in the profession as any manuscript of the later Wittgenstein. You might call the recording a sort of "self-bootleg," since Pete ultimately endorses this piracy. Originally captured in analogue, the thing finally showed up in digital form a few years back. I suppose that was inevitable.

Why has this music become the fabric of legend? I have heard tell that when he was President of the Southwestern Philosophical Society in the 1970s, he delivered his presidential address with his guitar in hand. Even if that's fiction, it ought to be repeated. The profession needs more tall tales than it currently possesses. The songs for which Pete is best known are mostly two-minute ditties, many of them parodies of show tunes, in which Pete places the doctrines and characters of the history of philosophy into comic settings. Different professors like different ditties, but among the perennial favorites are "Don't Blame the *Umgebung*," featuring a chorus sung falsetto from the standpoint of Peter Abelard, and the "Peloponnesian War Blues." The latter, being a fairly standard 12-bar, Delta blues number, contains one of the better internal rhymes I have ever encountered:

> They say if you religious, you'll burn old Sparta down
> If you believe in Jeeee-sus, you'll burn the Peloponneee-sus to the ground
> It never made much sense to me, to kill for Christ in 399 BC
> Don't wanna go down to Sparta and fight no Peloponnesian War

I don't see how that can really be improved on, either as a lament or as a commentary on Vietnam (which was the time when Pete wrote it). Thus, I recommend that the current book should be read with a willingness to share a secret irony with the storytelling uncle.

None of this is intended to lighten the very serious and very important contribution this book makes to getting Bergson straight. In many ways, it's about getting Gunter straight. The concern Gunter brings to the interpretation of Bergson is that of a multifaceted and accomplished person who, with a lifetime of effective activism and advocacy regarding environmental causes, has been able to use his command of science to make great changes in his part of the world, or as he would say, his neck of the woods. Pete has saved more of the woods, perhaps, than anyone since John Muir. Bergson helped him do that, along with a deeply informed orientation toward life, energy, and change. Gunter's full command of these ideas, along with a dozen others, made him persuasive as an advocate for conservation and building respect for nature. His significant literary ability and his voice in narrative have been no small part of his persuasiveness.

The uncle at the fireside is to be taken with great seriousness, and in a way that the dry as dust academic philosopher never will be. If Pete once sang a presidential address, one thing can be said for it: people remember it. And that is a part of what must be included in the rhetoric of philosophy, its form as communicated, its impact as a living meaning. Bergson had a similar gift. People *wanted* to read his books. And you will want to read this one.

And Pete Gunter is, without question, the most authoritative living source for Bergson interpretation. Indeed, one can place him with the four or five best in the history of this line of interpretation, with an extra palm added due to the historical distance Gunter enjoys and the access he has to subsequent developments in science. So, put another log on the fire, sit back, and enjoy this story. And tell it to your friends.

Works Cited and Consulted

Gunter's academic writings appear in the bibliography of the book. These are my sources for the introduction apart from those.

Bergson, Henri. *Creative Evolution*, authorized trans. Arthur Mitchell, intro. By Pete A.Y. Gunter (Lanham, MD: University Press of America, 1983).

_____. *Laughter: An Essay on the Meaning of the Comic*, auth trans. Cloudesley Brereton and Fred Rothwell (New York: Macmillan, 1913).

_____. *Matter and Memory*, auth. trans. N.M. Paul and W.S. Palmer (New York: Zone Books, 1988). In referring to this book, abbreviated MM, I have included in brackets the page numbers from the original edition and the Dover reprint, since these editions are more common than the Zone Books edition.

Gunter, Pete A.Y. "The Ceremonial Heap and the Smell of Burnt Gasket: Two Special Memories of Christmas," a short story in *A Texas Christmas: A Miscellany of Art, Poetry, and Fiction*, vol. 2, ed. John Edward Weems (Dallas: Pressworks, 1986). This story contains some more adventures of Jim Tremorgan and family, the protagonist in *River in Dry Grass*.

_____. "Justice's Fence," a short story in *New Texas*, ed. James Ward Lee (Denton: Center for Texas Studies, 1993). This story contains some more adventures of Jim Tremorgan and family, the protagonist in *River in Dry Grass*.

_____. *Nameless War*. Unpublished manuscript of a novel, provided by the author.

_____. *River in Dry Grass*, a novel (Austin, TX: Shearer Publishing, 1984).

_____. "A Stone for Samuel," a poem in *Southern Humanities Review* 4:3 (Summer 1970), p. 230.

Introduction

This study is an effort to resolve misunderstandings surrounding the thought of a particular philosopher, Henri Bergson (1859-1941). Once famous, his ideas have receded into the background of contemporary thought. There are many reasons for this eclipse. Changes in philosophical fashion, dramatic shifts in the zeitgeist, transformations of the sciences: all these have tended to relegate his thought – at least in appearance – to a far-off age. Such factors, I will argue, are secondary. The two most important obstacles to the understanding of this thought have been:

1. A serious misunderstanding of what he means by his central concept, intuition, and how it is intended by him to enrich our more analytic, often practical, thought and behavior.
2. A failure to understand the role Intellect plays in his thought. In spite of his repeated criticisms of intellect (sometimes termed reason or intelligence), he is thoroughly dependent on it.

As will become clear, intellect is for him a necessary condition of intuition: both of attaining it and, once attaining it, of expressing it.

A. A Few Preliminary Remarks

Before dealing with Bergson's concepts of intellect, intuition, and their interactions, it will be very helpful to say a few words about the main goals of this book. This will hopefully explain the structure of the present essay and its particular preoccupations.

One of the greatest problems in interpreting Bergson, as we will see, is the profound tension —some would say contradiction—at the center of his thought. On the one hand, there is the world of science: atomistic, mechanical, ideally reducible to points and instants, predictable. On the other, there is Bergson's world: fluid, continuous, creative, unpredictable. One seems to have two worlds, entirely distinct from the other. And, to quote Kipling, "never the twain shall meet."

B. Intuition-Analysis, Duration-Space

This impression of sharp dualism is profoundly misleading. If anything, it represents what Bergson was trying to escape, not what he was trying to affirm. The most important point to understand—the point to which the bulk of this study is devoted—is that the more dynamic side of his world, duration, the side which, he argues, science cannot grasp, enters into the other side enlarging its scope by making possible new modes of thought. Intuition, which for him participates in the flux of duration, fructifies: i.e. inserts creativity into its contrary.

The end result of Bergson's reflections is thus not a restatement of Cartesian dualism but an interactive duality in which the two sides reinforce each other. The less dynamic and creative side provides the resistance and the limits without which creativity would remain merely diffuse, unfocused. The more dynamic side, as I have said, creates new possibilities which transformed the less dynamic.

It is one thing to stress the interactive nature of Bergson's philosophy. But what did that philosophy actually achieve? The bulk of this essay shows that Bergson did actually achieve some important scientific successes: quite remarkable for someone presumed to be anti-scientific and by that very fact, anti-intellectual. Among these are his contributions to contemporary memory theory, to theories of biological time, to Louis de Broglie's wave theory of matter, to Jean Piaget's genetic epistemology. This book explores each of these along with others. The example of Bergson's theory of memory and its powerful influence on Marcel Proust is included in order to indicate that his approach is in no way limited to the sciences; on the contrary, it extends; the other components of human knowledge as well.

If this is true, Bergson's many applications of intuition to different aspects of our experience should have born fruit: should have opened up new vistas in the sciences and elsewhere. That is what the present volume attempts: to demonstrate, in some detail, that his insights did in fact enter into various components of science and make possible new discoveries. But the phrase "in detail" involves a problem which the reader should be warned of here. To deal any depth with a science much less with several sciences, as this essay does, is to write at some length about them. It may seem in what follows that in some areas this essay is concerned mainly with science, not with the French intuitionist himself. This is in no way true. But one cannot deal with the interrelations between philosophy and science without paying careful attention to the sciences themselves.

Two further points should be made before turning later to a more detailed discussion of intuition and intellect, duration and space. The first concerns the amount of attention which this book devotes—among the many sciences which are considered—to physics and the nature of matter. The second gives thanks to the many scholars who have helped dispel many of the misunderstandings of Bergson's thought to which I have drawn attention.

A significant part of the following essay will focus on the concept of matter and on the all-important notion of the hierarchy of durations in terms of which it must be understood. This emphasis might be thought to imply that the author believes that matter—the briefest of durations in Bergson's temporal hierarchy—is the most important of his ideas. This is not so. In his view, there are many levels of duration and all are important. But, once again, his concept of material duration has been, as he states, among the least noticed and the least understood of his ideas. It therefore merits careful reconsideration.

Finally, I do not mean to suggest that I am alone in trying to rescue Bergson for misunderstanding. Bergson scholarship has for some time now been laboring, often quite effectively, to remove obstacles to our understanding of the author of *Creative Evolution*. When one thinks, of an earlier generation, for example, of Milič Čapek. But there is a younger generation including John Mullarkey, Robin Durie, Susan Guerlach, Elizabeth Grosz, and Keith Ansell-Pearson among others. One would like to draw attention especially to the recent study by Mark Sinclair[1] which explores Bergson's ideas effectively and in depth. The reader will perhaps forgive me that after having studied Bergson's thought for many years along with the writings of these scholars, there are still a need to explore some points that have not been explored to add to the understanding of how Bergson sought, fruitfully, to bind together the disparate components of thought.

And so: To turn now to an examination of intuition, intellect, and their fruitful interrelations.

To deal effectively with the dramatic contrast between intuition and intellect it will be necessary to deal with another contrast: between duration and space. The object of intuition, Bergson states, is duration, the constant flow of things. The object of the intellect is space: geometry, quantitative measured time. One thesis of this essay is that the meanings (and uses) of intuition and intellect can only be made intelligible through a clear understanding of the structure of duration and its relations to space, which in his hands turns out to have a surprising structure of its own. If these are not understood, the relations which Bergson establishes between intuition and intellect will make little sense.

The nature of duration and of space are not apparent at first glance. They become apparent as one traces the development of his philosophy, which goes through a profound process of development. In his first writings, Bergson treats intuition and space as adversaries, each the enemy of the other. As we will see, these relations change precisely to the degree that the relations between duration and space, as he understands them, are transformed. Though he does

---

[1] Mark Sinclair, *Bergson* (London: Routledge, 2019), 324.

not give up the fundamental tension between intuition and intellect, he makes intuition dependent on intellect for its development and more, surprisingly, comes to understand intuition as able to nourish intellect, enabling it to fruitfully reformulate its fundamental concepts.

It would be pleasant if working all this out were a simple matter. By the very nature of the problems Bergson dealt with, this cannot be so. The problems confronted in this essay are many and complex, as, therefore, must be our treatment of them. The initial component of this essay will be two-fold. The first chapter will deal with Bergson's discovery of the stream of consciousness – of duration in its opposition to the static, non-temporal character of mathematical space and clock time. This discovery was to have positive consequences both for Bergson's later thought and for the future of philosophy. But, as we will show, it gave rise to consequences which contradicted both common sense and many of Bergson's own beliefs.

The second chapter will deal with Bergson's solutions to the problems raised by his early philosophy. If the first part of this chapter deals with the radical opposition of duration and space, the second part will deal with duration in and for itself. The end of this second chapter will be threefold, dealing in turn with 1. The question of the asymmetry of duration and the symmetrical terms by which Bergson chooses to describe it. 2. The problems involved in his concept of "rhythms of duration," a concept which became central to his later thinking. This notion involves the introduction into the concept of duration of what can be termed articulations or modes of discontinuity. Once these articulations are understood it is possible to explain how there can be different (that is, contrasting) "lengths" of duration which can be related to each other through the extension of more prolonged over less prolonged rhythms. This notion – of a continuity or hierarchy of durations – will be useful to Bergson in several respects. It is central to this essay.

It will, for example, help him make sense of 3, the problem of how the mind can objectively deal with the world around us. It will also make it possible for him to deal with the related mind-body problem. Finally, it will make it possible to find an entrance into problems of chronobiology (of biological time) and even of physics. Accompanying these problems is the question of degrees of spatiality, which Bergson introduces not only into his psychology but into his theory of matter. The mind, Bergson speculates, can extend by degrees into the world. It does not have to be, à la Descartes, excluded from space.

The author invites the reader to be patient. Perhaps Bergson's new "take" on the embodied subject will lead to resolutions of ancient problems: problems which will not relent until we try a new way.

I.

A Discovery and its Discontents:
Time and Free Will

A. Duration versus Space: Bergson's First Approach

The opposition between duration and space is presented in Bergson's first work, whose English title is *Time and Free Will*.[1] Here he makes his fundamental distinction between the time of consciousness and the time of clocks. It is interesting to see the context in which arrived at this distinction. Originally a disciple of the English philosopher Herbert Spencer, the young Bergson sought to make Spencer's thought more precise, by bringing it in line with the latest ideas of nineteenth-century physics. He paid particular attention to Spencer's concepts of space and of time. Here, he states, a surprise awaited him.[2]

The surprise came from a simple insight. Experienced time (i.e., duration) is not at all like our traditional measurable time. Experienced time "flows." Measured time is, paradoxically, static. It is made up of instants, which do not change. Similarly, for units of time, minutes or fractions of a minute, for example. Not only are such "units" static, but they are also homogenous. All time segments (for example, minutes or seconds) are the same in character as are all other time segments. But experienced time is not like this. No two moments of experienced time are identical. Each has its own unique quality, its own specific character. The same experienced moment will never come again.

Bergson meditated on the dramatic contrast between a time that flows and a 'time' made of static units. Where might it lead? What sense could he make of it?

For a philosopher who hoped initially to found a philosophy on an analysis of the fundamental ideas of physics, such questions must have been disconcerting. Previously, Bergson tells us, he had had little interest in psychology, with its

---

[1] Henri Bergson, *Time and Free Will*, trans. F. L. Pogson (London: George Allen & Ltd, 1950), 252. All future reference to this work will be cited in the text as TFW.

[2] Henri Bergson, *The Creative Mind*, trans. M. L. Andison (New York: Philosophical Library, 1946), 10. All future reference to this work will be cited in the text as CM.

"domain of the inner life."[3] Now he found himself obliged to study that domain – to explore it in ways he would not previously have imagined. The results were to be both interesting and original. He was to be one of the first to study the "stream of consciousness": psychology in its dynamic and active side. In doing so he was to open up new vistas in both psychology and philosophy, and elsewhere.

But if Bergson's study of inner time awareness can be reckoned a discovery, it led, as we have stressed above, to a number of vexing problems, problems firmly rooted in the sharp contrasts involved in his approach. What is the connection between the flowing of inner time and the static instants of clocks? How can there be an objective, measurable time in physics and the natural sciences if true time is subjective? And if there is a time "out there," how is it related to the unmeasurable fleeting time of inner consciousness?

Bergson's first book does not answer such questions. It would be more accurate to say that by systematically exploring the dramatic contrasts from which these problems arise, his original essay only makes such questions more evident and more pressing. Still, it will help to examine, however briefly, Bergson's initial explorations, the origins of his thought. This will make it possible to learn both how he was to formulate his earlier standpoint and how he, later, attempted to overcome it.

B. A Glance at Time and Free Will

Bergson's first major work, his dissertation, was originally titled not *Time and Free Will* but *Essai sur les données immédiates de la conscience* (*Essay on the Immediate Data of Consciousness*). The English translation of this work sidelines the original title, replacing it with *Time and Free Will*. If this title has the twin virtues of brevity and of signaling some of the conclusions to be drawn by Bergson, its original title, the *Essai*, has the all-important virtue of drawing attention to the fundamental problem which he faces: that of understanding the character of time as immediately experienced: the immediate data of consciousness.

Consider, he states, a pendulum. If I watch it, the pendulum is active – it moves, swinging. The pendulum thus exhibits succession: one motion happening **after** another. But, Bergson argues, when we treat the pendulum mathematically we substitute numbers for perceived oscillations. We do this in two ways: either by summing them up or treating them singly.[4] If we sum them up, we conclude

---

[3] CM, 12.
[4] TFW, 105.

there are sixty oscillations. But the number does not exhibit a succession. Its parts are given simultaneously.

This is equally true if we pick out a particular oscillation, terming it "one." One, like sixty, contains no hint of succession. If I experience oscillations in succession, Bergson adds, that is because I experience them in my own psychological time, where succession reigns. On this subjective basis, he insists, we bind together the successive swings of the pendulum,

> ...each permeating each other and organizing themselves like the notes of a tune, so as to form what we shall call a continuous or qualitative multiplicity with no resemblance to number. I shall thus get the image of pure duration.[5]

The swings of the pendulum or any rhythmic succession are perceived by us, then, as a kind of qualitative gestalt, a "rhythmic organization of the whole."[6] Apart from our human mode of consciousness, however, do clocks, pendulums and other apparently mobile features of the world endure in the world as we do? In spite of appearances, Bergson insists, they do not. In counting the swings of the pendulum or following the hand on a clock dial we are not summing up duration, we are merely "counting simultaneities."[7] He insists:

> Now, let us withdraw for a moment the ego which thinks these so-called successive oscillations: there will never be more than a single oscillation, and indeed only a single position of the pendulum, and hence no duration. Withdraw, on the other hand, the pendulum and the oscillations: there will no longer be anything but the heterogenous duration of the ego.[8]

The result is striking. In the ego, there is "succession without mutual externality." But in the so-called "outer" world there is the opposite: "mutual externality without succession."[9]

Those familiar with the history of philosophy will recognize this opposition between an unextended mind and a geometrical, extended world. It was introduced into modern philosophy by its founder, René Descartes. It forms, even today, the basis of many discussions of the so-called mind-body problem. Descartes' famous dualism, however, is based on the contrast between space

---

[5] TFW, 105.

[6] TFW, 106.

[7] TFW, 108.

[8] TFW, 108.

[9] TFW, 108, 116, 120.

and non-space, extension vs non-extension. Bergson's starting point is based on the contrast between duration and non-duration. Descartes continued to defend his dualism to the end of his career. Bergson, by contrast, seems to hesitate. His early approach to the fluid inner and the static outer world puzzles him.

No doubt, he argues, "... external things change, but their moments do not succeed one another, except of a consciousness which keeps them in mind."[10] But this won't do. He has just identified change with succession. How is it possible to suppose change in which there is no succession – when succession is, so to speak, the very backbone of change (i.e. duration)? Aware of the insufficiency of his first effort to resolve the puzzle, he tries a second:

> Hence we must not say that external things endure, but rather there is in them some inexpressible reason in virtue of which we cannot examine them in successive moments of our own duration without observing they have changed.[11]

But the appeal to an inexpressible reason does not help. What is it? How does it help us to resolve the problem? If it cannot be expressed, it cannot be assigned any meaning.

A second problem with the early Bergsonian dualism lies in his treatment of freedom: of the free act. Such acts, he argues, stem from processes in the depths of the self, processes of which we are not ordinarily aware. When we try to make up our mind about some important choice, he states, we may seem to be considering clear, definite possibilities. However,

> ...below this most reasonable pondering over advice, something else, was going on – A gradual heating and a sudden boiling over of feeling and ideas, not unperceived, but rather unnoticed.[12]

But even though our elders or friends may offer what appears to be bits of reasonable advice,

> Something may revolt against it. It is the deep-seated self, rushing up to the surface. It is the outer crust bursting, suddenly giving way to an irresistible thrust.[13]

---

[10] TFW, 227.

[11] TFW, 227.

[12] TFW, 169.

[13] TFW, 169.

That is, the free act does not arise *ex nihilo*, at an instant. It is the product of personal history. When we examine that history, we realize that we had shaped our ideas, lived those feelings,

> ...but that, through some strange reluctance to exercise our will, had thrust them back into the darkest depths of our soul...[14]

The free act, then, though scarcely guaranteed *a priori*, is the result of a continuous process, a dynamic series of states that "permeate and strengthen one another."[15]

Bergson's account of the free act was to have a significant influence, for example, on subsequent French Existentialism. The problem is that on his terms there is no way to understand how this act can be expressed in behavior. Even pushing a button or clicking a computer mouse takes time and involves succession. But succession on his terms does not exist in the outer world. It seems then that the free act cannot be embodied in the world. It remains bottled up in the self.

A third problem with the early Bergsonian dualism is that, as stated in *Time and Free Will*, it places the human mind, including the human intellect, outside of nature. This had been done intentionally by René Descartes. It was accepted by many of his successors, most prominently Immanuel Kant and the idealist tradition which followed. For all its easy acceptance by modern philosophers, it is a very strange idea. Bergson, like many of his contemporaries, found it especially hard to reconcile with biological evolution, which finds man's conceptual abilities to have developed precisely through an interaction with the physical and social world around us. In Bergson's next study he will follow this latter, naturalistic, view of the mind and of man's relationships to nature. In doing so he will upend and transform many of the fundamental suppositions of his first work.

---

[14] TFW, 169f.
[15] TFW, 170.

II.

Rethinking Duration:

Matter and Memory

A. Personal Memory

This chapter deals with a fascinating topic: the nature of personal memory. The author cannot resist starting a discussion of it with an example drawn from his recent experience. A few months ago, he was walking down a street in Denton, Texas when, suddenly, he found himself transported to a very busy road over two hundred miles away in Houston. That is, he suddenly found himself walking down Washington Avenue, a street where he had not been in over half a century. The subtropical light, the 1940's cars and pickups were, while they lasted, vivid: a full technicolor world, including the sensation of walking. The flashback lasted little more than a second, while the image remained vivid for several weeks: vivid and, the author must admit, haunting.

Why the memory of that not-at-all important experience, depicting a street where I had never spent much time, on a long-ago day that was not particularly important? In spite of much reflection, I have not been able to answer that question. But there is another, a far more profound question that seems even harder to resolve: How is it that the memory – a very rich, detailed memory – of an obscure and not very significant experience can be preserved over so many years? Its preservation suggests that not just our important experiences, whether traumatic or triumphant, are preserved in memory. Rather, it is that all or most of our experience is preserved.

That, indeed, is Bergson's position. All memories are preserved, constituting an astronomical amount of reminiscence. This is, if one thinks about it, an outrageous claim. There are many facts to support it. But to explain what Bergson means by it will be necessary to make some distinctions. These are found in his second book, *Matter and Memory*, published in 1896.

There are, Bergson states, two forms of memory. The first he terms habit memory.[1] Habit memory is put in place by effortful repetition and has little to do with the past *per se*. I am able to recite the alphabet or the multiplication

---

[1] Henri Bergson, *Matter and Memory*, trans. N. M Paul and W. S. Palmer (New York: Zone Books, 2005), 80, 82-83. (All future references to this work will be cited in the text as MM.)

table simply through ingrained habits and with no reference to past experience. Habit memories, Bergson adds, are ingrained in the brain and nervous system

The second form of memory he terms spontaneous memory.[2] Spontaneous recollection, he argues,

> …is perfect from the outset; time can add nothing to its image without disfiguring it; it retains in memory its place and date.[3]

It constitutes the author's recollection of a long-ago Houston street. It records events in their richness, with remarkable detail. It is not, like habit memory, contained in the brain. Contemporary psychologists term it epochal memory.

Much psychological evidence supports the capacious nature of epochal memory. Recent experiments at the University of York support its inclusiveness. Professor Rob Jenkins and his group, convinced of the importance of memory of faces, questioned a group of twenty-five subjects about how many people they knew personally and whose faces they could remember. On average participants listed 40 people in the first five minutes and 21 in the final five minutes. The team concluded that participants would have listed 549 people if they were given unlimited time. Other tests involved the recognition of photos of famous people. These led researchers to the conclusion that most people can recall about 5000 faces.[4] It is safe to say that most of us do not know that we carry such a large rogue's gallery with us. But, on Bergson's terms, 5000 faces are but a miniscule sample of the mass of detail that makes up personal memory.

A second experimental study referenced as well in a recent special issue of the *New Scientist*[5] also relates to the character of epochal memory. The previous article cited above demonstrates the retentive character of personal memory. "What is Memory For?" deals with another, equally important aspect of it: the part which it plays in enabling us to deal with the future.[6] The author states that although we are likely to view memory only as the recalling of information,[7] memory theorists find an entirely different and equally important function for it. That is, there is a strong link between being able to remember past events

---

[2] MM, 81-83.

[3] MM, 83.

[4] "Our Memories are Packed with Thousands of Mugshots," *New Scientist* 240, no. 3200 (October 20, 2018): 17.

[5] The special section begins with "The Grand Memory Illusion," *New Scientist* 240, no. 3201 (October 27, 2018): 31–32.

[6] "What is Memory For?" *New Scientist* 240, no. 3201 (27 October 2018): 32-33. (All future references to this item will be presented in the text as NS.)

[7] NS, 32.

and being able to plan for the future."[8] This thesis has two empirical, factual supports. Patients with brain damage who suffer impaired personal memory are also impaired in imagining the future. In addition, imaging studies show that similar patterns of brain activity underlie both.[9] If we are unable to recall past events and preferences, "our ability to make sound decisions crumbles also."[10] This is so because during the decision-making process we use previous choices and existing knowledge to assess options and imagine how they might turn out. We will discover that this is precisely Bergson's point.

B. Proust and Memory: Developing an Intuition

The notion of spontaneous or epochal memory may seem merely interesting: a quaint and perhaps intriguing idea. In fact, it has had a fruitful and useful career. This is very much in keeping with Bergsonian intuition, which begins as a simple insight which then develops into complex applicable conceptual structures. Beginning with the realization that memory is an active and global phenomenon, Bergson, as we have seen, goes on to distinguish kinds of memories and describe the ways in which they function. At least two major applications were to derive from his insight. The first was *À la recherche de temps perdu*, Marcel Proust's immense exploration of personal memory. The second was the creation of modern memory science, via the work of Endel Tulving, Daniel Schachter, and their colleagues.

Since the appearance in 1922 of *Du côté de chez Swann*, the first installment of Proust's massive million-and-a-half-word novel, there has been a running debate over the extent to which Bergson's thought influenced Proust and in what respects. I do not wish to enter into the details of this fascinating discussion. Instead, I would like to concentrate on a single and undeniable point. One cannot go in search of lost time unless one is convinced that it still exists and can still be found. That is exactly what Bergson's notion of spontaneous (epochal) memory did for Proust. Bergson, to repeat, contends that all personal memories are preserved – ***all***, not a few. He holds this position and insists on it. Proust, besides being a personal friend of Bergson's (and a second cousin of his by marriage) had read *Matter and Memory*–consulted it at crucial points while writing his novel.[11]

---

[8] NS, 32.

[9] NS, 32.

[10] NS, 32.

[11] Pete A.Y. Gunter, "Bergson and Proust: A Question of Influence," in *Understanding Bergson, Understanding Modernism* (New York: Bloomsbury, 2013), 157-176.

It is this contention, of the integral conservation of the past, that "grounds" Proust's masterpiece. It is highly doubtful whether he would have proceeded without it. It is hard to imagine what *À la recherche du temps perdu* would have been like without it.

If Bergson and Proust are in entire agreement concerning the survival of the past, in another they stand radically opposed. That is, as we have seen, for Bergson the retentiveness of memory has as its covert purpose to allow us to function in the present and to create our futures.[12] For Proust, by contrast, the goal of literature is to explore the past *per se*. Bergson is vectored towards the future; Proust towards the past.

C. Bergson and Memory Science

Besides its influence on twentieth century literature, Bergson's notion of spontaneous memory makes an appearance in the sciences. In 1973 the psychologist Endel Tulving introduced and with his student and later collaborator, Daniel Schachter, developed Bergson's distinction between two major forms of memory.[13] His championing of this distinction had two benefits. First, it made possible a far more complete list of the kinds of memory than had been available previously. Prior to Tulving's intervention psychologists had only one significant distinction to apply in their researches: that between long-term and short-term memory. This notion, introduced by H. Ebbinghaus,[14] was helpful. But it did little to help researchers deal with the varieties of mnemonic experience: that is, the many different kinds of memory. In turn, the elaboration of the kinds or types of memory made it possible to correlate them with specific brain regions and specific complexes of behavior. There could thus be a full-fledged science of memory where before there could only be more or less scattered research.

Fortuitously this development coincided with the burgeoning cognitive science revolution. The two viewpoints could thus fruitfully reinforce each other and increase insight into the many phenomena of memory. Among other factors, psychology and neurophysiology, which had previously been studied separately[15], could now be studied together.

---

[12] See NS, quoted above.

[13] Pete A.Y. Gunter, "A Tale of Two Memories. Bergson and the Creation of Memory Science," *Memory & Matter* 11, no. 2 (2014): 137-152.

[14] H. Ebbinghaus, *Über das Gedächtnis* (Leipzig: Duncker und Homblot, 1885).

[15] Astonishingly, it seems to me.

Tulving's two memory systems nicely parallel Bergson's distinction between spontaneous and habit memory and were proposed with an awareness of Bergson's contributions. It was exciting, Daniel Schachter notes, to contemplate using scientific techniques to study concretely what Bergson and others had observed in the clinic and had theorized about.[16] Tulving, Schachter and their colleagues were to take the Bergsonian distinction between conscious remembering and learned habits (conceptual habits included) and place them in a new experimental and psychological context.

This appropriation of a philosophical distinction by scientific researchers was in no way the dogmatic imposition of an *a priori* dogma. It was, and was intended as, an insight which requires conceptual imagination and flexibility to be developed. For those familiar with the concept, it resembles far more a Kantian "regulative concept" than an <u>a priori</u> concept arrived at (as in, for example, Descartes' philosophy) by deduction.

It is true that Bergson, in distinguishing between spontaneous and habit memory, does not define, as contemporary memory theorists do, the different kinds of habit memory. But in defining habit memory he makes it clear that it includes a diverse spectrum of neurophysiological mechanisms.

Thus, he states that there is only a difference of degree, not of kind, between the so-called perceptive faculties of the brain and the reflex functions of the spinal cord.[17] His treatment of the brain, particularly of the effects of brain damage on the use of words and on the varieties of mental illnesses make it clear that he had studied brain physiology including localization. Hence, the five-tiered hierarchy of contemporary memory theory (episodic memory, working memory, semantic memory, procedural memory, and representational memory) would have come as no surprise to him. Nor would the fact that these factors function together, not as separate systems.

---

[16] Daniel Schachter, *Searching for Memory* (New York: Basic Books, 1996), 169-170.
[17] MM, 225.

III.
Rhythms of Duration

Bergson's theory of epochal memory influenced and played an important role in the creation of Proust's novels and in contemporary memory science. It would not be hard to show that is had other impacts as well: for example, in the development of the stream of consciousness novel.[1] What follows is an effort to show how it also leads to a purely philosophical idea: rhythms of duration. This idea, in turn, has implications for the sciences. I will put off discussions of these until later. For now, I will discuss the appearance of this idea in *Matter and Memory* and speculate on how Bergson came to formulate it.

The term "rhythm of duration" does not appear in *Matter and Memory* until page 201, four fifths of the way through his text. Why it makes this late appearance is a puzzle. Its introduction follows a discussion of the nature of matter,[2] a discussion which concludes by rejecting the accepted corpuscular-kinetic (Newtonian) notion that matter consists of hard, inert particles moving in an empty space. Rather, Bergson argues that matter consists

> ... as we have foreshadowed, precisely in the immense multiplicity of the movements which it executes within itself. Motionless on its surface, in its very depths it lives and vibrates.[3]

This, with its implications for our views of motion, space, and substantiality, it is intended to provide the beginnings of a plausible durational interpretation of the physical world. But before discussing this possibility, it will help to examine the notion of rhythms of duration itself. The term "vibrations" may seem synonymous with "rhythms of duration." In fact, it is only a particular case. Bergson applies it only to the behavior of matter.[4] The phrase "rhythms of duration" has the wider connotation. It applies to duration in all cases, at all

---

[1] Shiv Kumar Kumar, *Virginia Woolf and Bergson's 'Durée'* (Hoshiarpur, India: Vishveshvaranand Book Agency, 1957), 17; *Bergson and the Stream of Consciousness Novel* (London: Blackie, 1962; New York: University Press, 1963), ix, 174. For further references to Kumar Cf. the Bergson bibliography, 1986.

[2] MM, 202-205.

[3] MM, 204.

[4] MM, 138, 202-205, 208, 228, 229, 248.

levels.[5] As such, it appears in his later books, *An Introduction to Metaphysics* (1903) and *Creative Evolution* (1907).

Perhaps the clearest and most effective way of understanding rhythms of duration is by directly comparing them: that is, to understand them through their interrelations. Music presents us with innumerable examples. All are based on the fundamental relationship, of "extending over." If a song is sung while a guitar is strummed, the musical phrases of the song extend, temporally, over the tempos marked by the guitar. If, to take orchestral music, a theme played by the trumpets extends over a briefer theme reiterated by the woodwinds and this theme, in turn extends over the beats of a drum, one has a threefold example of temporal extending-over. Ideally, there is no limit to the number of extendings over, or to the rhythmic complexity of music.

Music is only one case of temporal "layering." In a crowded restaurant, one will often encounter a conversation proceeding in long slow phrases temporally extending over a rapid almost staccato discourse taking place at a nearby table. What is true for music and conversation is equally true of physiology. The phrases of slow breathing often extend over more rapid heartbeats. The rhythms of walking extend over the beating of the heart as the longer rhythms of brain waves preside over briefer rhythms in the brain.

Overlapping temporality becomes a fundamental feature of Bergson's thought – a fact that is all too easy to overlook. We all know the old canard. "Time flies When You're Having Fun." The banality of this old saw should not blind us to its significance. Human temporality, Bergson points out, occurs at different levels, literally: broader, richer durations extending over briefer, less rich durations. It exhibits varying tempos.

In an all-important passage of *An Introduction to Metaphysics*,[6] he makes this clear. The intuition of duration, he insists,

> …far from leaving us in the void as pure analytics would do, puts us in a contact with a whole continuity of durations, which we should try to follow either downwardly or upwardly: in both cases we can dilate ourselves by a more and more vigorous effort, in both cases transcending ourselves. In the first case, we advance towards a duration more and more scattered, whose palpitations, more rapid than ours dividing our simple sensation,

---

[5] MM, 201, 203, 205, 207-208, 216, 220, 222, 228, 247, 248.

[6] *Introduction to Metaphysics* originally appeared independently. It was later included in *The Creative Mind (La pensée et le mouvant)*. Future references will be marked as CM.

dilute its quality into quantity: at the limit would be the pure homogenous, the pure repetition by which we shall define materiality.[7]

It is hard to exaggerate the centrality of this passage, both to the argument of *An Introduction to Metaphysics* and to the cosmology and biology of his next work, *Creative Evolution*. In *An Introduction to Metaphysics*, it is intended both as a summing up of the analyses of the temporality of experience which precede it and the enumeration of the characteristics of metaphysics that follow it. That is, metaphysics, for Bergson, is a highly reflective study of the specific levels of duration, reaching from "higher limits" to "lower": "Between these two extreme limits moves intuition, and this movement is metaphysics itself."[8] This approach allows metaphysics a great deal of specificity. If there are unique levels of duration *each can be studied on its own*. Intuition must focus on specific levels of temporality in and for themselves.

The passage just quoted is interesting for another reason. It is a piece of phenomenology. But unlike other forms of phenomenology, it escapes the clutches of the transcendental ego and reaches out into the world. From the side of human awareness, it is an intense highly focused form of consciousness. From the side of the world it reaches into a series of increasingly brief durations: durations possessed by actually existing things. Here Bergson attempts to escape the cage within which Descartes had imprisoned modern philosophy: the encapsulation of the mind in a subjective prison from which there is no exit. Bergson makes his exit from his durational *cogito* into the world. For him we literally participate in the rhythms of the world.

Besides the phenomenological nature of this text (i.e. "between these two extremes moves intuition…") there are texts which extend his thought from our experience to speculations on the nature of biology; that is, to speculations concerning the temporal structure of living things. Thus, in *Matter and Memory* Bergson insists that there are:

> … many different rhythms which, slower or faster, measure the degree of tension or relaxation of different kinds of consciousness and thereby fix their respective place in the scale of being.[9]

This suggestion appears again on the next to last page of *Matter and Memory*, where it is related directly to biological evolution:

---

[7] CM, 221.

[8] CM, 121.

[9] MM, 207.

...the progress of living matter consists in a differing differentiation a function which leads first to the production and then to the increasing complication of the nervous system capable of canalizing excitations and of organizing actions: the more the higher [brain] centers develop, the more numerous become the motor paths among the same excitations... [This] allows the living being to choose, in order so that it may act. And even greater latitude left to movement in space –this is indeed what is seen. ***What is not seen is the growing and accompanying tension of consciousness in time.***[10]

This passage, besides affirming the centrality of the notion of varying tensions (levels) of consciousness in time, makes a start at relating the temporal varieties of our experience to biological evolution and the structure of the brain. Bergson here is making his first steps towards the immense biological and temporal panorama of *Creative Evolution*. But he is also beginning to sketch the relations between biological evolution and human freedom. Without the human brain and central nervous system, he will argue, human freedom is impossible. Human neurophysiology makes possible a broad variety of choices for human beings. Without this complexity freedom would have no basis.

---

[10] MM, 248. My additions in brackets; the emphasis is mine as well.

IV.

From Duration to Biological Time

A. Pierre Lecomte du Noüy, Alexis Carrel

So far it has been possible to show that Bergson has developed a phenomenology of inner time consciousness which attempts to escape limitation to "inner" consciousness. Rather, its goal is to reach out via the staircase of descending durations to the lowest level of duration, physical matter. Bergson does not describe how many steps there are in the staircase. The important point is that there are many, and that his celebrated "intuition" is capable –in fact required—to halt at specific levels and explore these. The results of this would be, ideally, to broaden the focus of intuition. It would also be, in the process, to arrive at insights which could be useful or, better, fruitful. We have seen that this was true for the Proustian novel and for the creation of memory science. In what follows, I will examine the researches Pierre Lecomte du Noüy and Alexis Carrel in biological time. The intended result --to repeat myself-- is to explain how Bergson's approach could give rise to insights which are applicable outside of philosophy: in this case, in biology.

While serving as an officer in the First World War, Pierre Lecomte du Noüy (1883-1947) began making visits to Field Hospital No. 21, just outside of Compiégne. Alexis Carrel, the head of the hospital, soon recognized the young man's intelligence and ability and asked him to study a problem which had been troubling him: the nature of the cicatrization (healing) of wounds – no small problem in a war in which more soldiers died from infection of wounds than from the wounds themselves. Specifically, Carrel asked Lecomte du Noüy to find a geometric equation giving the rate at which wounds heal. Relieved of his duties in the French army, he became a full-time resident in the hospital. He now possessed a massive resource in the wounds of the soldiers there and began work.[1]

Lecomte du Noüy did not have an easy time with his project. He did not have an orthodox scientific education and was not particularly strong in mathematics. Nonetheless he persevered. The carnage of World War One provided plentiful wounds of all ages, depths, and configurations to study. The end result was two equations: These predicted the rate at which wounds heal, taking into account

---

[1] Russell G. Foster and Leon Kreitzman, *Rhythms of Life* (New Haven: Yale University Press, 2005), 213-231. All future references to this work will be cited in the text as RL.

wound size and shape, the age of the wounded person and other factors.[2] His thesis, "Experimental Researches and Applications of Measurement and Calculation to a Biological Phenomenon: Cicatrization,"[3] was presented in June 1917 at the University of Paris. An odd commentary on the state of biology at that time was the highly negative response of biologists on his committee. These, untrained in mathematics and suspicious of it, opposed his thesis bitterly. Only under pressure did they give way and allow the thesis to be accepted.[4]

Lecomte du Noüy's results were fascinating. He was able to show that wounds heal according to two factors, the size of the wound and the age of the patient. Small wounds heal more swiftly than large ones in proportion to their area. The extent of healing can be predicted using his index of cicatrization. Interestingly, if the healing process is halted, it will accelerate to make up for lost time. Analogously, if the activity of one its two components (the epithelial and connective tissue, respectively) is slowed, the other component will accelerate its activity to make up for it. The cicatrization process thus acts as if it had a timetable to keep up with and valid alternative resources to fulfill it.

The effects of aging on the healing of wounds were revealing. If a wound of 20 cm^2 heals in 20 days for a six-year-old, it heals in 31 days if the subject is 20, 41 days if he is 30, 78 days if he is 50, 100 days if he is 60. Such wounds thus heal five times faster for a child than for a 60-year-old.[5] The practical results of these discoveries (beyond their effect on the French army's way of dealing with wounds) were straightforward. If a wound was not healing according to its timetable, it would be clear that something was amiss. This would spark a search for the negative factors involved.

Lecomte du Noüy draws several conclusions from his studies of physiological time. One is that living things have an accelerated tempo which differs from the regularity of clock time. It took him several years to move from this realization to the notion of a general biological time. His concept of biological time was similar to Bergson's, though not identical to it. It is hard to believe that Bergson's

---

[2] P. Lecomte du Noüy, *The Road to Human Destiny*. (New York: Longmans, Green, and Co, 1955), 304-306. All future references to this work will be cited as RHD. The first i=s-s1s(t+√T and s2=s1[I-it+T] where s=initial wound surface, s1= the surface t days later, s2 the surface T days later, and i an index of cicatrization.

[3] Pierre Lecomte du Noüy, "Recherches éxper. et applie. des méthodes de la mesure et de calcul à un phénomène biologique: la cicatrisation." Thèse Ac. Sc. Paris, Dec 18, 1947. Printed Paris: Gauthier Villars

[4] RHD, 89.

[5] Pete A.Y. Gunter, "The Heuristic Force of Creative Evolution," *Southwestern Journal of Philosophy* 1, no. 3 (1970): 111-118.

ideas were without influence on Lecomte du Noüy. He had long been preoccupied, we are told, with the problem of how matter could be understood apart from its temporality.[6] The problem if the cicatrization of wounds had, fruitfully, been posed to him in temporal terms--What is the rate of healing?--by Carrel, whose acquaintance with Bergson and his ideas predated his acquaintance with Lecomte du Noüy and whose adherence to Bergson's philosophy was scarcely a secret. At the least, one can postulate an indirect influence.

Lecomte du Noüy's book, *Biological Time*[7] was published in 1936. It is quite instructive to read Bergson's response to it.

> I have just read *Biological Time* that you were good enough to send me and I wish to tell you how much your book has interested and taught me. Your experiments your general views on cicitrization which form its main thesis would alone suffice to make your book an important one. But you do not stop there. On these precise observations and reflections you have grafted a new concept of physiological time which I believe, is sound and fruitful and which leads you to interesting considerations on time and general. All my congratulations.[8]

Bergson's recognition of the nature of Lecomte du Noüy's research and its similarities to his own standpoint is not surprising. What is interesting from a point of view of the present essay is its general support of Bergson's position. That is, it provides corroboration for his contention that the whole organism embodies a fundamental temporality which must be taken into account. If Lecomte du Noüy had studied cicatrization as part of physiology, there remained many other aspects of physiology which could be studied *sub specie durationis*. Just as Carrel studied cellular and tissue cultures from the same point of view, there remained many other temporally-oriented research is cytology which would be undertaken. The intuition of duration, supposedly anti-scientific, could form a basis for viable research programs.

And so, we come to Alexis Carrel. For all their long and close association, Lecomte du Noüy and Carrel were very different personalities. Lecomte du Noüy, modest and painstaking, guarded his privacy. Carrel was endlessly and very effectively self-promoting. (His face appeared on the cover of the September 16th, 1935 *Time Magazine*.) He was a polymath, working in many areas. His

---

[6] RHD, 89.

[7] Pierre Lecomte du Noüy, *Le temps et la vie* (Paris: Gallimard, 1936), 268. In English, *Biological Time* (New York: Macmillan, 1937), 180; in the most recent reprint, *Biological Time* (Andesite Press, 2015), 200.

[8] RHD, 187-189.

discovery of a method for suturing blood vessels won him the Nobel Prize for Medicine or Physiology in 1912.[9] He was also a pioneering transplant surgeon,[10] an investigator and theorist (as we have noted) of tissue culture,[11] and a student of biological time.[12] He was also among the first to apply the new motion picture technology to study the behavior of the tissue culture and cells.

It would help to know more about Carrel's and Bergson's personal relations. We know that Bergson gave a banquet for Carrel at his home in 1912 on the occasion Carrel's winning the Nobel Prize.[13] We also know that on a trip to the United States he was to visit Carrel's laboratory at the Rockefeller Institute.[14] There were doubtless other interactions between the two men. In any case there can be no doubt about Carrel's embrace of Bergson's philosophy. It was total. ***The organism***, Carrel stated bluntly, ***is duration***.

It is not possible in this essay to examine Carrel's work in detail. Rather, the author will limit this discussion to a survey of Carrel's general notion of biological time and to his use of movies (microcinematography) to study cells and tissue culture. Alex Comandon was the first to film tissue cultures, using Carrel's method for fragmenting and externalizing the cells of complex bodies.[15] Carrel returned the favor, using Comandon's microcinematography to study techniques for growing somatic tissues outside the body. Carrel's and Comandon's films were not kept a secret. They, along with accounts of their contents, circulated widely for many years.[16]

Carrel's approach to the study of cells and tissue turned out to be very useful. In the words of Andrew S. Reynolds, it helped "prove the viability of cells outside

---

[9] G.M. Lowrie, "The Scientific Contributions of Alexis Carrel," *Clinical Cardiology* 10, no. 7 (1987): 428-430.

[10] David Hamilton. *The First Transplant Surgeon: The Flawed Genius of Alexis Carrel* (New York: World Scientific, 2016), 580.

[11] J.A. Witkowski, "Alexis Carrel and the Mysticism of Tissue Culture," *Medical History* 23, no. 3 (1977): 279-296. The author notes that Carrel's methods for studying tissue culture were elaborate and repetitive, like those of the alchemists. Hence, mysticism.

[12] Alexis Carrel, *Man, the Unknown* (New York: Harper and Row, 1935), xv and 346; *L'homme, cet inconnue* (Paris: Plan, 1935), 400. All future references to this work will be cited in the text as MU.

[13] Jacques Chevalier, *Entretiens avec Bergson* (Paris: Plon, 1959), 254-256.

[14] Isaac Benrubi, *Souvenirs sur Henri Bergson* (Paris: Delachaux et Niestlé, 1942), 125-126.

[15] Hannah Landecker, "Cellular Features: Microcinematography and Film Theory," *Critical Enquiry* 31, no. 4 (2006): 2.

[16] Heinz Rosenberger, Carrel's technical assistant, produced Carrel's movies for publication. Cf. Bryan M. Stramer and Graham A. Dunn, "Cells on Film: The Past and Future of Cinemicroscopy," *Journal of Cell Science* 128, no. 1 (2015): 9-13.

the body and provided an unmatched window into the life of the cell."[17] Hannah Landecker describes Carrel's films as revealing not merely the things constituting life but the previously unobservable processes of their lives.[18] Jimena Canales concludes that the use of film was essential to the development of 20th Century cell biology.[19]

It is easy to see why prior to the new approach biologists had to be content with stained specimens on glass slides and with pen and ink sketches of cells, tissues, organs, and with microscopic photographs. If these were useful, they were nonetheless static. Carrel's approach (and for that matter, Lecomte du Noüy's) pulled physiology and cytology out of statics and into dynamics.

Another result of this transformation was a renewed interest in function as a dynamic property of life. Cells, Carrel protested, are not so many construction bricks stacked to comprise an organ or tissue. They are active. Their behavior sustains living things. Carrel, therefore, called for a 'new cytology' which could both take these factors into account. Carrel insists:

> ...the unsatisfactory nature of our knowledge of the elements of the body must undoubtedly be attributed to the conception on which classical histology is based. Whether dead or living, dissociated on a slide explant in a drop of plasma, or sectioned and stained, cells and tissues have been considered as inert forms, unrelated to their environment and deprived of functional activity. They have been extracted from both space and time.[20]

Obviously, he concludes, the traditional viewpoint has to be given up and replaced by another set of concepts "containing a greater part of truth." To do so will be to return to the close observation of "the concrete event which the tissue is."[21]

I will conclude this brief general sketch with three points. The first involves the continuing usefulness of microcinematography. The second, which must be included in any balanced account of Carrel's work, is his mistaken view that cells, tissues, and organs are potentially immortal. The third is an overview of

---

[17] Andrew Reynolds, *The Third Lens: Metaphor and the Creation of Modern Cell Biology* (Chicago: Univ of Chicago Press, 2018), 88.

[18] Landecker, 2.

[19] Jimena Canales. "Dead and Alive: Micro-cinematography Between Physics and Biology," *Configurations* 23 no. 2 (2015): 235-251.

[20] Alexis Carrel, "The New Cytology," *Science* 73, no. 1890 (20 March 1931): 297.

[21] Ibid.

the capacity of Bergson's viewpoint to inspire research like those of Lecomte du Noüy and Carrel.

The use of film to study biological processes did not end with, nor was it confined to, the work of Carrel and his associates. Applications of Carrel's inspiration continued in a number of fields. The photomicrographs of R.G. Canti were essential and convincing both scientists and the general public of the power of radiation treatment of cancer and materially aided cancer research, the later researches of Michael Abercrombie were instrumental in establishing the mechanisms of cell movement, including cell migration.[22] Brian M. Stramer and Graham A. Dunn make a strong case for the future of this technique. To the qualitative observations of early practitioners have been added new technologies (phase-contrast microscopy, laser-scanning confocal microscopes, multiphoton microscopy, and many others).[23] These researchers significantly improve numbers. That is, they make it possible to perform remarkably accurate mathematical analyses of their subject-matter analyses, not previously available.

If Carrel's methods were able to prepare the way for future breakthroughs, it does not follow that he made no mistakes. As we've stated above, Carrell believed that the organs and tissues he was able to keep alive outside of the organisms were potentially immortal. Barring negative interference, they could and should live forever. In one case, a collection of fibrolasts lived on for 30 years (in a broth derived from chicken embryos) until the experiment was ended after Carrel's death.[24] It was not until the 1960's, however, that his belief in immortality of tissues was decisively falsified. This was established by biologist Leonard Hayflick, who discovered that telomeres, the endpoints of chromosomes, ceased to function after a limited number of chromosome replications (in some cases 50.) scarcely the indefinite series postulated by Carrel. Without functioning telomeres, the transmission of genetic information ceases to take place.[25]

---

[22] Stamer & Dunn, "Cells on Film," 8-9.

[23] Ibid 11-14.

[24] David M. Friedman, *The Immortalists: Charles Lindbergh, Dr. Alexis Carrel and Their Daring Quest to Live Forever* (New York: Harper Collins, 2008), 352.

[25] J.A. Witkowski, "Dr. Carrel's Immortal Cells," *Medical History* 24, no. 2 (1980): 129-142. Also, L. Hayflick, "How and Why We Age," *Experimental Gerontology* 33, no. 7-8 (1996): 639-653.

V.

Bergson's Expanding Space:
His Cosmology

What has been said so far introduces Bergson's notion of duration as a series of successive pulsations or rhythms and these rhythms as having greater or lesser breadth. This in turn makes it possible to explain one way in which such rhythms can coexist: mainly, by "extension" of one over the other, a relationship which can be reiterated *ad indefinitum.* (As noted above, there can be any number of such temporal overlaps, depending on the complexity of the phenomena under study.) There can also be rhythms contemporary with each other, beating out the same rhythm: e.g. two electrons separated in space but having the same frequencies: two drummers beating out the same tempo.

As we have seen, towards the end of *Matter and Memory* Bergson extends this notion of temporal overlap into biology, postulating that the higher or dominant species sustain richer and broader rhythms of duration. Pierre Lecomte du Noüy and Alexis Carrel, as we have also seen, extend the notion of duration to the component parts of the organism. Not just the organism as a whole but its cells, tissues, and organs sustain fundamental rhythms. They exhibit and sustain **many** such temporalities.

There are two ways of approaching such "continuities" (Bergson's term) or "hierarchies" (my term) of duration. The first describes their creation, their dynamic coming-to-be. The second portrays them, once having come into existence, as "stable" with different levels of duration functioning so as to sustain them. The first involves not only phenomena exhibiting human creativity. It also involves such phenomena as physical cosmology and biological evolution. To these I will now turn, starting with cosmology.

When he was working out the details of his relativistic cosmology, Albert Einstein confronted a troublesome problem. Is the universe stable: unchanging in its fundamental structure? Or does its structure change with the passage of time? Einstein consulted scientists. They (the majority of the physics community) agreed that the universe remains essentially unchanged, and Einstein went along with them, introducing the famous "cosmological constant" into his equations. Henceforth, all agreed, the universe would, thanks to Einstein's constant, exhibit a sober steady state. Above all, it could never begin at time "t." Nor could it expand.

It is, then, interesting to note that in his *magnum opus, Creative Evolution* (1907), Bergson proposes that the physical universe does in fact expand. This expansion he traces back to initial creation. The result is the first proposal of a "big bang" cosmology. This idea was later developed by Charles Lemaître, in 1927,[1] and still later, through the work of Edwin Hubble and others, has become the reigning paradigm in physical cosmology. It is ironic that Bergson, whose ideas have regularly been branded as "antiscientific or "anti-intellectual," should have been the first to propose such an idea.[2]

Bergson arrived at his cosmological speculations through very different preoccupations than those of later cosmologists. He was fascinated with the implications of the second law of thermodynamics. According to the second law, put technically, energy becomes increasingly unavailable to perform work. Thus, to take an often-used example, if I strike a match, the light and heat given off will, along with the chemicals released, be dispersed into space, never to return. The result is a charred remainder of what was highly structured wood. Originally formulated in terms of the loss of heat energy, the second law was broadened to cover the loss of all forms of energy. Later formulations also construe it in terms of the loss of information.[3]

Bergson termed the second law "the most metaphysical" of the laws of science because it depicts the overall process of nature: the direction in which nature is going. But it follows from the fact that nature is moving towards increasing disorder in the future that in the past it possessed a higher degree of order than it has now. Bergson postulated not a state of perfect order at the beginning of the universe but an initial act of creation which marks its birth. That is, our universe is not always existed. It was born. Since then it has increasingly "detended"[4] into space dispersing to create both myriad physical particles in the small and various stellar objects (solar systems, nebulae) in the large.

Bergson's dynamic cosmogony is easy to overlook – has, in fact, been almost universally overlooked because of its speculative, admittedly metaphysical character, and because of the widely shared belief that metaphysics and

---

[1] Lemaître has only recently been given credit for his hypothesis. Cf. "Cosmic Law Renamed to Expand Credit," *Science* 362, no. 6414 (2018): 504. The International Astronomical Union has renamed the constant describing cosmic expansion the Hubble-Lemaître Law. No influence of Bergson on Lemaître has been discovered. It is possible.

[2] Pete A. Y. Gunter, "Bergson's Theory of Matter and Modern Cosmology," *Journal of the History of Ideas* 32, no. 4 (1971): 525-543.

[3] Léon Brillouin, *Science and Information Theory*, 2nd ed. (New York: Dover Edition, 2013), 354.

[4] CE, 130, 135.

science do not mix; or at best make a very unfortunate mixture. Admittedly Bergson's account of "The Ideal Genesis of Matter" is hard to follow.[5] Mixed with its account of the cumulative "detension" of matter are arguments involving the nature of space, of being and non-being. These in turn involve references to contemporary astronomy, and, above all, analyses of the status of the laws of thermodynamics.

In spite of the involved nature of his argument, the end result is clear. Matter is not something that simply exists. It is created via a process that embodies increasingly brief rhythms of duration, ending in rhythms of extraordinary brevity. Thus, at the limit,

> ... we get a glimpse of an existence made of the present which recommences unceasingly—devoid of real duration, and nothing but the instantaneous which dies and is born endlessly. Is the existence of matter of this nature? Not altogether, for analysis resolves it into elementary vibrations, the shortest of which are very slight durations, and most vanishing, but not nothing.[6]

One way of putting this is to say that matter is never fully spatialized. It is never simply a point at a location. It always has temporal breath. And it always has spatial extension. That he had a concept of smaller and smaller spatial stretches or "parts" is often not understood, though it is essential to his standpoint, as I have stressed. It parallels and is a fundamental component of both his psychology and his metaphysics. This notion of space or "extensity" is unorthodox. That is, he holds that spatiality (the extensions of material things) is not given all at once but by degree. Things become increasingly spatialized. Whether there is a three-dimensional static space waiting to be filled is put into question.

---

[5] The problem with analyzing Bergson's text at this point is simply that he had not decided at the time he wrote *Creative Evolution* whether the scientific evidence supported belief in a single universe with a single process of detention-expansion or a "multiverse" containing a number of such expansions. The evidence suggests that he was later to conclude that he came to accept the former thesis, i.e. that the universe is one and that it has a single mode of transition, the creation of matter and of space. This is seen in *Duration and Simultaneity* in which he argues strenuously that the universe has a single duration.

[6] CE, 129.

VI.

Bergson, Fractal Geometry, and
the Peculiar Nature of Space

Luckily for Bergson, a new mathematics has appeared which, in different ways, helps substantiate his viewpoint. This is fractal geometry, which utilizes the notion of fractional or incremental space and its companion notion, self-similarity. These concepts provide Bergson's notions of levels-of-duration and space-by-degree with conceptual content. That is, they help explain what the philosopher means. Equally, through its successful application in any number of fields, fractal geometry suggests that its constructs are not just imaginative mathematical ideas. They tell us something about the world.

In what follows I will give a brief account of fractal geometry. This account, among other things, will involve the notion of degrees of spatiality which Bergson introduced much earlier into philosophy. My description of fractals will end with a sketch of "L-series" fractals, whose branching structure nicely parallels not only the divergent character of biological evolution as Bergson describes it but many examples of creativity and of biological structure.

The term fractal was introduced in 1975 by Benoit Mandelbrot who, by bringing together a number of "mathematical monsters," that had been ignored or even shunned by the mathematics community, created a new science. [1]

It would be nice if fractals constituted a small, manageable subject matter or even if the term "fractal" had a simple definition. Neither is true. Fractal geometry has, since Mandelbrot's first work, enjoyed a remarkable development. Yet, puzzlingly, the term fractal turns out, unlike Euclidean geometry or set theory, to lack a classical definition. For most mathematicians an object is a fractal if it exhibits most of the following properties:

1. Fine structure (detail at all scales)
2. Self-similarity (made up of smaller and smaller copies of itself)
3. Simple recursive construction

---

[1] Benoit Mandelbrot, *The Fractal Geometry of Nature* (New York: W. H. Freeman and Company, 1983). All future references to this work will be cited in the text as FGN.

4.   Size dependent on the scale at which a thing is measured.
5.   Classical methods of mathematics and geometry are not applicable.[2]

The classical methods of mathematics and geometry are suited for and demand, among other things, single clear definitions. Again, the features of fractal geometry do not.

To this author, one of the most surprising results of fractal geometry is the realization that space need not have numerical dimensions. An example of this between-the-dimensions geometry is provided by the Koch curve which I will briefly discuss.

The Koch curve can be described offhandedly as a line attempting to become a surface and not succeeding. To create a Koch curve, one divides a straight line into three equal parts. One then erases the middle section and replaces it with two sides of an equilateral triangle. The construction continues through the continued addition of proportionally smaller incomplete equilateral triangles. Thus, for the next step, repeat this recursion again, once more with proportionally smaller triangular shapes. The reader can perhaps imagine how complex the resulting line will become in even a few more steps. This is another of the surprising characteristics of fractal geometry. From Doric, simplicity by simple constructions ends with Rococo exuberance.

In the case of ordinary Euclidean geometry, size has no impact on dimensionality. If we "shrink" a line to one-third of its original length it fits into the original line exactly three times. Similarly with an ordinary square. Shrink it to one-third of its original length and one gets a square that fits into the original square nine (that is, 3x3) times. The same holds of a cube constructed on the foundation of the original square. The relative size in each case varies. The dimension remains constant. In the words of Richard Elwes:

> For the 1 dimensional line the smaller (line) fits into the original line 3-1 times. For the 2 dimensional square it fits in 3x3 times, that is 3-2. For the three dimensional cube it fits in 3x3x3 times, that is to say 3-3.[3]

In each case the exponent depicts a simple dimensionality: one for the line, two for the square, three for the cube. Each is an obliging whole number: d=1, 2, or 3.

It would be a mistake simply to equate Bergsonian duration with fractal figures. His extension is dynamic and qualitative. It vibrates with life. Fractals, by contrast, are geometrical, hence static. Even so, both in its scaling and in its

---

[2] Kenneth Falcone, *Fractals: A Very Short Introduction* (Oxford: Oxford University Press, 2013), 7-8. All future references to this work will be cited in the text as F.

[3] Richard Elwes, *Mathematics Without the Boring Bits* (New York: Metro Books, 2011), 60.

partial extensity, Bergson's hierarchy of durations strongly resembles Mandelbrot's new geometry. So far as I know, Bergson is the first person, philosopher or mathematician, to argue that actual, concrete space (i.e. extensity) is "between the dimensions": it never is congruent with the dimensions or classical Euclidean space but at best "approximates" them.

It might be objected that on one point Bergson's durational hierarchy is not consistent with fractal hierarchy. A fractal hierarchy continues ***ad indefinitum***. But Bergson's temporal hierarchy has, as he points out, a stopping point. There is, he postulates, a lower level of duration as of spatial division. For him, the hierarchy ends there.

The inconsistency, however, is only apparent. Mathematical (or "perfect") fractals are readily distinguished by mathematicians from natural fractals. The former proceed indefinitely. The latter have lower limits, and often exhibit fractal form in an incomplete or imperfect way. Cauliflower, for example, presents a case of fractal self-similarity. But its fractal pattern terminates after only a few repetitions. The coastline of Britain, to take Mandelbrot's famous example, exhibits self-similarity of an approximate pattern with approximate scaling.[4]

---

[4] Benoit Mandelbrot, "How Long is the Coast of Britain?" *Science* 156, no. 3775 (1967): 636-638.

VII.

More on Fractal Geometry

A. Divergent Fractals, Divergent Evolution

What has been said so far about fractals barely scratches the surface of a complex subject. Equally, it by no means goes deeply into the relations between Bergson's thought and the different sorts of fractals. To remedy these two lacks I will discuss the diversity of fractals, and then stress the similarity between Bergson's treatment of biological creativity and the L series (that is, series that represent "branching" fractals). Branching fractals have been used with remarkable success to describe biological structures. They are, it turns out, strikingly analogous in structure to Bergson's accounts of all sorts of creativity: genetic, biological, artistic.

The Koch curves are among the simplest of fractal constructs. For one, they represent only one fractal family, the geometrical fractals. Besides these there are also the far more elaborate algebraic fractals which include Julia sets. These are closely allied to the famous Mandelbrot set, proclaimed by its advocates to be the most complex object in mathematics. There are several different fractal dimensions. Hausdorff dimensions are the most used and consulted.[1]

The notion of branching (or ramification, or bifurcation) is familiar: so familiar that no one ever thought to construct a mathematical structure on its basis or to map its articulations. The centrality of the notion of branching in Bergon's philosophy becomes clear in *Creative Evolution*, where he depicts branching as fundamental to biological evolution. Albert Vandel points out that Bergson was among the first to stress evolution as divergent, not convergent[2]. Not all those seeking a panoramic description of evolution have agreed. Teilhard de Chardin, for example, has argued that all evolution tends towards an ultimate convergence: an omega point which sums up the purpose or

---

[1] Those interested in pursuing the diversity of fractals might consult a recent Wikivisually article on the subject. "List of Fractals by Hausdorff Dimension." https://wikivisually.com/wiki/List_of_fractals_by_Hausdorff_dimension. Accessed 15 Feb 2022. The authors of this article compile an impressive list of fractals by Hausdorff dimension.

[2] Albert Vandel, *L'homme et l'évolution*, 13th ed. (Paris: Gallimard, 1958), 47.

significance of the evolutionary process.[3] Not so Bergson. If evolution does converge at some points, the basic nature of evolution is to diverge, creating distinct life forms (as we have seen, plants versus animals, vertebrates versus invertebrates, reptiles versus mammals, etc).

This ramifying picture is not limited to evolution. It is found everywhere in living organisms, in the transition from the fertilized egg to the adult organism, in the transitions from the precursors of the various organs and organ systems to the functioning organs and systems themselves. That is, both genetics and embryology like evolution itself are focused on the varieties of ramifying biological processes. Bergson goes on to ascribe such processes to human social evolution, hence to human artistic, technological, and religious creativity.[4] It is essential, as we have seen, to his physical cosmology: that is, in the diverging processes which create subatomic particles at one limit, astronomical objects at the other.

A couple of things should be pointed out about Bergson's divergent concept of creativity. First, it is not teleological (purposive). As I have just stated, it does not converge to a preordained point and is not constructed according to some preconceived plan or blueprint. Not only does it divergence and diverge again, surprisingly and unpredictably, rather than filling in the blanks of possibilities previously inscribed in the nature of things. It ***creates possibilities***.[5]

Thus, if there is an archetype which presides over the Bergsonian universe, it is not that of any particular biological species or art form or astronomical structure. It is that of ramification itself. For Bergson, to use Gilles Deleuze's term, reality is inherently rhizomatic.[6]

Two other "archetypes" appear in Bergson's thought, as I have implied. These are the scaled nature of existence and the structure of the durations which make up this scale, whether at a macro-level (as in his cosmology) or the micro-level (as in his description of the brief pulsations which make up matter).

---

[3] P. Teilhard de Chardin, introduction to *The Phenomenon of Man*, by Julian Huxley (New York: Harper and Row, 1961), 318.

[4] In case there may be any doubt that Bergson takes this position, his text makes it clear. Evolution, he insists, diverges (CE, 66, 87, 115, 163); dissociates (CE, 76, 163, 167); subdivides (CE, 173); occurs in "scissions" (CE, 158,163); diverges (CE, 66, 163), bifurcates (CE, 65), and splits (CE, 87).

[5] Pete A.Y. Gunter, "Bergson's Creation of the Possible," *SubStance* 114, no. 36 (2007): 1-9.

[6] Gilles Deleuze, *Bergsonism*, trans. H. Tomlinson and B. Haberjam (New York: Zone Books, 1991), 142.

The fractal approach which describes branching or ramified processes is termed the "L-series."[7] The L-series has some remarkable characteristics. It can generate a number of general botanical forms simply by constructing them *a priori*: palms, maples, willows, mimosas. So far as this writer knows, no Pythagorean ever claimed so much for geometry. The L-series also has applications to animals. Three of these applications will be described here: the lungs, the circulatory system, and the skeleton. Fractal mathematics does not merely describe these structures and their generation. It describes them in extraordinary detail.

The structure of the lungs is familiar. Starting from the bronchae, they repeatedly split into smaller and smaller tubes until after about eleven branchings they arrive at the alveoli, which pass oxygen into the bloodstream and allow carbon dioxide to be absorbed. In the words of Kenneth Falconer:

> Adult human lungs are about twelve inches long and five inches wide, but because of their branching fractal structure have an enormous fractal surface area of about one hundred square yards.[8]

What fractal geometry has added to our knowledge of the lungs is precision. Fractal structure achieves an enormous area within a confined space, allowing oxygen to be supplied to the blood with remarkable efficiency.

Closely similar fractal branching occurs in the circulatory system. As it transports blood from the heart to all the parts of the body arteries divide into successively narrower arterioles. These in turn divide to form capillaries of roughly 0.01mm diameter. For this system to function, every cell in the body has to be within 0.1mm of a red blood vessel. In human beings, the total length of the system of arteries and veins is a staggering 60,000 miles.[9] The branching structure of the circulatory system, like that of the lungs, has been known for a long time. The use of fractals, as in the case of the lungs, has made it possible to study this system with precision and to explain how it is capable of functioning with such efficiency.

Similarly with the skeletal system. It has long been a puzzle as to how bone can exhibit both stiffness and toughness: strength and flexibility. The answer is

---

[7] This collection of fractals is named after Aristid Lindenmayer, a Hungarian theoretical biologist. See P. Przemslau and A. Lindenmayer, *The Algorithimic Beauty of Plants* (New York: Springer-Verlag, 1990), 189. Also, from the series *Lecture Notes in Biomathematics*, see *Lindenmayer Systems, Fractals and Plants*, with contributions by A. Lindenmayer, F. D. Frachis, R. Krithivasan (Berlin: Springer-Verlag, 1989), 116.

[8] F, 107.

[9] F, 105.

found in a recent study which demonstrates that its mineral organization is hierarchical at the nanoscale. The authors conclude:

> ...bone (as a material, as a tissue, and as an organ) follows a fractal-like organization that is self-affine. The assembly of bone components into nested helix-like patterns helps to explain the paradoxical combination of enhanced stiffness and toughness of bone...[10]

Few would have thought that anything as solid and apparently amorphous as bone would turn out to be a tightly organized hierarchy of mathematical structures, or that these structures could be conceived as rhythmic in nature.

---

[10] N. Reznikov, M. Bilton, L. Lari, M.M. Stevens, and Roland Kroger, "Fractal-like Hierarchical Organization of Bone Begins at the Nanoscale," *Science* 360, no. 6388 (2018): 507.

VIII.

Duration and the Structures of Life:
A First Look at Bergson's Biology

When Bergson in *An Introduction to Metaphysics* postulates a scale of durations reaching from that of human consciousness to the extraordinarily brief rhythms of matter, he postulates an entire philosophy of nature. He does not attempt to describe the contents and the character of this *Weltbild* in detail, at each scale. We do get some help, for example, by looking at his accounts of physical cosmology and of biological evolution. But to fill in the details we are left with the necessity of exploring a number of relevant sciences in terms of their temporality and of using some imagination: enough to focus clearly on applicable results.

In this chapter, I will explore the implications of Bergson's concept of nature for three closely related sciences: chronotherapy, chrononeurology, and chronobiology[1]. The author believes that if Bergson's philosophy or some philosophy like it (that of Alfred North Whitehead, for example, or of William James) had been widely accepted in the early twentieth century, these three sciences would be far more developed than they now are.

A. Time in Medicine: Its Relevance to Everything

We inhabit a planet that turns on its axis every twenty-four hours: a fact that has profound implications for the creatures that live here. Human beings like other earth-bound organisms are profoundly involved in the earth's daily cycles. These roughly 24-hour cycles are termed circadian rhythms. They serve as a temporal ordering principle, establishing the basis for our sleep-wake cycle, blood pressure and body temperature cycles, and much else. Besides circadian cycles, there are ultradian (briefer than twenty-four hour) and infradian (longer than twenty-four hour) rhythms. All three cycles affect and are affected by each other. All are strongly involved in the maintenance of health, including mental health.

---

[1] Chronotherapy is often termed chronomedicine. Both chronotherapy and chrononeurology (sometimes termed neurochronology) can be construed as components of chronobiology. Here I find it useful to treat those fields as distinct sciences. One can add chronopharmocology as a subfield of chonomedicine.

The extent that we are dependent on these rhythms and their mutual coherence (their synchrony or "synch") is only now beginning to be understood. This is particularly evident where our natural bodily rhythms come into conflict with and are disabled by artificial temporalities imposed by our society. Jet lag and shift work cycles are now beginning to be recognized as destabilizing the body's (and mind's) rhythmic cohesion. Equally important, we have been slow to realize that the timing of the medicines we take may be more important than whether we take these medicines at all. These realizations form the basis for a dawning subfield of chronomedicine: that is, chronopharmacology.

Chronopharmacology has been slow to take root in American medicine. The reasons for this are many. In their historical study, *Rhythms of Life*, Russell G. Foster and Leon Kreitzman argue that one of the basic reasons for this--- besides sheer ignorance---is the difficulty researchers in the field find in producing clear, unequivocal (hence, clearly useful) results. In the competition for funding, chronopharmacology (like chronomedicine generally) easily gets elbowed aside.[2] It is especially gratifying, then, that the 2017 Nobel Prize in Medicine was awarded to three circadian rhythm researchers who discovered a "clock" protein that builds up in cells in certain times of day and breaks them down in others. In mice, nocturnal creatures, the clock protein (acetaminophen) builds up at night and breaks down in the day. When a large dose of acetaminophen is administered in the morning nothing negative happens. When the same dose is administered at night, serious damage occurs to the liver.[3]

Foster and Kreitzman, in their plea for the recognition and institutionalization of chronotherapy,[4] are able to cite several instances in which research into medication and its timing has been successful. In 1976 George E. Rivard began treating children suffering from leukemia with anti-cancer drugs including 6-MP (6-mercaptopurine). When he looked into his data several years later he discovered that children who took 6-MP at night were three times more likely to have their cancer go into remission than those who took it in the morning. Rivards's realization had an effect, leading doctors to prescribe 6-MP at night.[5] In cancer therapy this can be extremely important. Drugs given for cancer can have serious negative side effects (on the heart or the kidneys for example). The

---

[2] Russell G. Foster and Leon Kreitzman, *Rhythms of Life* (New Haven: Yale University Press, 2005), 213-231. All future references to this work will be cited in the text as RL.

[3] George Szasz, "It's Time for Chronomedicine," *British Columbia Medical Journal* (27 June 2019), http://www.bcmj.org/blog/it-s-timechronomedicine. Accessed 10 Jan 2022. Also, R. C. Huang, "The Discovery of Molecular Mechanisms for Circadian Rhythms," *Biomedical Journal* 41, no. 1 (2018): 5-8.

[4] RL, 212-231.

[5] RL, 223.

basic challenge in cancer treatment is to kill the tumor without killing the patient. By taking account of the chemistry of cell cycles, it has proved possible to determine when to give cancer therapy medicine with less damage to non-cancerous cells. One benefit of this case of applied temporality is that it is then possible to give more of the medicine.[6]

This subheading (subchapter) could be continued at great length. The relevance of chronomedicine to bodily rhythms is a difficult subject. But enough has been said to indicate the relevance of process philosophy (Bergson's thought, but not only Bergson's) to this field. Besides the examples cited above, research into Alzheimer's disease, forms of arthritis, asthma and heart disease have been shown to be closely involved with the body's temporality.

B. Time and the Brain: Chrononeurophysiology, or Neurophysiology as Music

The materials in the following two sections, on the layered, multistoried architecture of the brain and on the dual functions of the hippocampus, will be well known to those familiar with neurophysiology. They may wish to jump to later sections or, simply to scan what I have written, and move on. For those to whom neurophysiology is less familiar an apology is still in order. What I have written about the scaled (and rhythmic) structure of the brain will have some aspects of a classroom lecture or a scientific dictionary article. The aim in these two sections is to show the value, including the fruitfulness, of Bergson's approach. There is no way of doing so without, somewhat prosaically, covering the relevant facts as they are currently known.

The human brain is a waxy substance little bigger than a grapefruit. Unfortunately for our theories this lumpy mass turns out to be by far the most complex object the human mind has ever encountered. It should not come as a surprise, then, that we have a hard time understanding it. What should come as a surprise is how many contemporaries write as if they fully understood the brain and how soon they are going to solve the "hard problem": namely that of how the brain gives rise to the (presumably insubstantial) mind.

The study will make use of Gyorgy Buzsaki's *Rhythms of the Brain.*[7] Remarkable for its insights into the breadth of the problems brain scientists encounter and its knowledge of the relevant literature, Buzsaki's study provides a clear and effective overview of chrononeurophysiology as it is now being pursued. He admits the limitations of his essay, which does not deal with the function of the

---

[6] RL, 217.

[7] Gyorgy Buzsaki, *Rhythms of the Brain* (Oxford: Oxford University Press, 2006), 448. All future references to this work will be cited in the text as RB.

spinal cord and brainstem, which limits itself to the mammalian brain, and confronts alternatives only when necessary. Even so, he draws a clear conclusion:

> Rhythms are an essential part of normal brain operation and my goal is to convince the reader that neuronal oscillations, both beneficial and deleterious, are a fundamental physiological brain function.[8]

Insight into these factors will result not only in a better understanding of how the brain works but will achieve progress in the treatment of pathologies stemming from pathological rhythms.

For all his immersion in empirical detail, Buzsaki is also a theorist. He comes to his work with a general conceptual standpoint, one at least partially familiar to the readers of this essay. That is, he is profoundly influenced by fractal geometry and its close kin, the physics of chaos (often cited as complexity theory). The notion of complexity is fundamental to his program. Its similarities to the Bergsonian viewpoint are striking.

We recall Bergson's basic assumptions:

1. The universe, from top to bottom is comprised of duration: rhythms of duration.
2. These structures are ordered in terms of "overlap." The longer durations overlap the briefer, resulting in a scale or hierarchy of durations.
3. Though the content of these durations will vary along with their intensity, they have the same structure, at all levels.
4. Bergson's scale of durations is thus self-similar and can be termed "fractal."
5. In tandem with fractal geometers Bergson holds that there is no unitary spatial dimension. The lower limits of his rhythmic scale approximate ordinary 3D space but do not attain it.

Much more needs to be said about Bergson's rhythms of duration. They are not externally related. Each is influenced by their predecessors and can influence briefer and be influenced by "higher" or "lower" rhythms of duration in a hierarchy. If these factors are not taken into account, both Bergson's (and Buzsaki's) descriptions of the brain will be incompletely understood. Buzsaki's interpretation of the brain parallels the first four of these assertions.[9] That is he interprets the brain as first of all comprised of rhythms and dynamic structures

---

[8] RB, 27.

[9] Buzsaki does not deal with the problem of fractal dimensions. Nor does he show an interest in questions of internal relationships. He does, however, insist that structures at one scale of the fractal hierarchy can influence those at other scales. "Higher" components of the brain, he holds, can and do influence lower, and vice versa.

(neuronal loops) composed of rhythms. These rhythms are organized vertically, in a series.

> No matter what fraction of the brain we are investigating neuronal loops are the principle organization at nearly all levels. A physicist would call this multilevel self-similar organization a fractal loop.[10]

These parallel temporal layers or loops Buzsaki continues, perpetually interact with each other (RB34). This set of fractal levels with its hierarchical structure is inevitable, he concludes, because complex systems represent "multiple nested levels of organization."[11]

This is a long way from the straightforward mechanical models which most of us have learned from textbooks. Not only does Buzsaki propose a scaled, rhythmic notion of the brain; he depicts a neural system which involves "sensitive dependence on initial conditions" and hence strong elements of unpredictability.[12] He argues that the complex networks of the brain have memory--that is, firing patterns of neurons are constrained by the "*entire past history*" of their networks.[13] Those familiar with Bergson will also recognize in Buzsaki the distinction which the French philosopher draws between the anti-entropic course of evolution and the downward drift of matter. That is, the Hungarian scientist distinguishes clearly between "disorder-destined" physical systems and "order-centered" brain dynamics.

To return to the fractal scaling of the brain: on the large (macro) scale it is threefold: 1. the reptile brain[14] (which developed before reptiles and mammals diverged in their evolutionary paths) 2. the allocortex or limbic system[15] and 3. the neocortex (the higher or superior structure capping the brain).[16]

Buzsaki accentuates this scaling, noting for example that the neocortex itself has six layers, stacked vertically. While not neglecting the rest of the limbic system or allocortex, he focuses his attention on the hippocampus,[17] a part of the limbic system profoundly involved in two seemingly opposed and unrelated functions: the structuring of spatial location and the processing of personal

---

[10] RB, 30.

[11] RB, 52.

[12] RB, 63.

[13] RB, 127. Emphasis is Buzsaki's.

[14] Consisting of the olfactory bulb, brainstem, cerebellum, mesencephalon, and basal ganglia.

[15] Consisting of the amygdala, hippocampus, entorhinal cortex, and hypothalamus

[16] RB, 278-280.

[17] RB, 279. More accurately, he focuses his attention on the hippocampus and the closely related dentate gyrus.

(epochal) memory. He treats the hippocampus, though it is separated from the neocortex or upper brain, as a "giant cortical module." The hippocampus is thus a "single large multilayer space," constituting through its vertical connections.[18] That is, it contains, like the cortex, multiple vertical layers.

> The vertical structure, it should be noted, does not prevent communication between its many levels:
> Integrative neocortical operations emerge through interactions between the modules rather than within single isolated modules.[19]

They are part of a system of oscillators within an intricate relationship between the various rhythmic components.[20]

This verticality is omnipresent in the brain, but it's the exact number is impossible to determine. The important point to stress is Buzsaki's insistence that the temporally "stacked" layers and sublayers of the brain constitute not only a spatial, but (as noted earlier) a temporal scale. It is the brain's rhythmic behavior which makes possible its highly complex functions. For Buzsaki, without the rhythmic temporal behavior of the cortex, the hippocampus, and much more, thought would not be possible.

Though much is not known about "superimposed and ever-growing loops" (RB280) it is clear that the principle direction of the neocortex-paleocortex is upward to the neocortex (RB282). Brain function is, for Buzsaki, essentially cumulative.

C. Time and the Hippocampus: An Odd Duality

The question of how the hippocampus can be deeply involved in the preservation of personal (episodic) memory and at the same time engaged in the formulation of geometrical place/location is much debated in contemporary neuroscience. In the context of a book that examines the process philosophy of a philosopher like Bergson, it is particularly interesting that a scientist is able to offer an answer to this question based centrally on the rhythms of duration.

The Key to the puzzle lies, Buzsaki states, in the theta rhythms of the hippocampus and its entorhinal context. Theta oscillators ordinarily behave as a single monolithic oscillator[21] beating out a sustained rhythm as the animal engages in the same behavior.[22] They thus provide rhythmic background which, if its

---

[18] RB, 185.

[19] RB, 45.

[20] RB, 119.

[21] RB, 173.

[22] RB, 308.

rhythms vary even slightly will lead to the generation of interference. This in turn can create "spike timing"[23] which affects the oscillations of place cells involved in specifying a geometrical location.[24] Temporality, surprisingly, can be involved in the specification of its opposite: place.

It would be quite natural if our episodic memories of our surroundings were to accompany and reinforce our cerebral mapmaking, thus enable us to more effectively engage in "getting around" in the world. Not only are the neuronal mechanisms of episodic memory and spatial navigation analogous,[25] we now have evidence that the hippocampal entorhinal system is involved in both episodic and semantic memories.[26] Memory representations, he argues, may well have evolved along with mechanisms involved in spatial navigation.[27]

D. Chronobiology in General

This chapter has begun with discussions of applications of the concept of duration to medicine and to the study of the brain. A critic might argue that this was a poor starting point, that this chapter should have begun with a study of biological time in general. The writer feels the force of this objection. But he hopes that by starting with a discussions of chronomedicine and chrononeurophysiology, he will both whet the reader's curiosity and provide the reader with ideas necessary to understand the many-sided concepts of biological temporality. He also hopes that this approach will make it easier to show how Bergson's ideas mesh quite naturally with current scientific discoveries.

We have already dealt at several points with Bergson's notion of duration. It forms the basis of his philosophy of nature and, as the writer has repeatedly stressed, involves a scale of durations reaching from the human stream of consciousness to the brief pulses of matter. If this is true, most of the rhythmic temporality which makes up Bergons's world lies in the levels of duration between human awareness and that of matter. These are occupied by living things, each of which Bergson, as we have seen, describes as having its own unique temporality. But the scaling of durations does not stop there. Each organ

---

[23] RB, 314.

[24] RB, 161; 296-301.

[25] RB, 318.

[26] RB, 327.

[27] RB, 333. The author cannot resist pointing out again that in developing his distinction between episodic and habit (now termed semantic) memory, Bergson concludes that one of the most important functions of episodic memory is to help us recognize our surroundings and deal with them, including our sense of location and place.

of a living thing, he argues, has its own rhythmicity as does each component of the organism: all the way down to the cells (and to unicellular organisms).

Bergson persists in reaffirming this view of things. First put forward in *Matter and Memory*, it is reaffirmed in *An Introduction to Metaphysics* and *Creative Evolution* and again in *Duration and Simultaneity* (1921) his critique of relativity physics.[28] There can be no question that this is his *Weltanschauung*.

The trouble is that we have trouble seeing the world in these terms. The "real" world is after all ---at any rate to all appearances---a world of solids. The trees across the street, the courthouse in the distance, the cars passing by, all are surely commonsense bodies with definite boundaries and stable structures. Who would doubt it? To push the commonsense argument further, what is to be gained by looking at the world in any other way? The architect knows that he or she is not dealing with a fluid medium. The mechanic knows how to repair a car without resorting to metaphysics. And we know that matter (to which the tree can be "reduced") is made of hard, inert particles.

Bergson's response to this objection is developed throughout his writings, running parallel to his investigations of the nature and structure of duration. The problem is, he insists, that the picture one gets while looking across the traffic into the trees is not innocent. It is a function of the kind of creature that we are more than an ultimate representation of what things are like. The senses leave out, exclude more than they take in.[29] They leave out the universal interaction of things, focusing on and isolating particulars, leaving out dependence on physical environment. Thus, the familiar "things" of our world. In this we sin in two ways: one, in neglecting dependence of a thing on environment and, two, in constituting "things" out of hard, inert particles while ignoring both their durational contents.

A goal of philosophy for the French intuitionist is thus to get beyond the simple pictorial images of our ordinary life and gain insight into the rhythmic continuity which underlies them. He is clear that this will require an effort. We are genetically programmed to deal with particulars as solids and motion as a series of positions. Inverting this habitual direction of thought will he states, require an effort.

---

[28] Henri Bergson, *Duration and Simultaneity*, 2nd ed., trans. L. Jacobson (New York: Bobbs-Merrill Company, 1965), 46. All future references to this work will be cited in the text as DS.

[29] Bergson takes a closely similar view of the brain's function in memory, i.e. that of focusing on a few memories while excluding many. In both cases, the failure to exclude would render memory and perception totally ineffective.

Another way of putting the problem is to admit that Bergson's view of the world seems initially strange: rhythms here, rhythms there, rhythms everywhere. It will seem less strange if it is seen that he is not putting forth the picture of the world as a bizarre mélange of rhythms. Rather, he believes that the rhythms of nature, as stressed throughout this essay, exhibit a fundamental order. He also believes that to study and to come to understand this order is to arrive at new concepts which will be more accurate and, as I have also stressed, more useful.

When Bergson wrote at the end of the 19th and the beginning of the 20th century his panrhythmic view of life no doubt appeared odd: (rhythm here, rhythm everywhere) a philosopher's fantasy. Yet today this is increasingly the view taken by biologists. Circadian twenty-four rhythms, to take the best known and most researched example, are indeed everywhere: in the organism as a whole and in its organs, and even its cells and in unicellular organisms. There is not just one circadian rhythm, as I have pointed out, but many, involving the sleep-wake, body temperature, hormonal release, etc.

As noted above, in addition to circadian rhythms there are swarming multitudes of less than twenty-four-hour ultradian oscillations. In an article that considers the possibility of a multilevel biological clock, Diego A. Golombek and his colleges list eleven of these. [30]

1. sound localization
2. motor control
3. speech generation
4. speech recognition
5. playing music
6. dancing
7. foraging
8. decision making
9. learning
10. heartbeat
11. fine tuning of endocrine secretion.

The situation here is the same as the attempt cited above, to list kinds of fractals. That is, the authors make it clear that their lists are systematically incomplete. Too much new is being discovered. Another example should be

---

[30] Diego A. Golombek, Ivana L. Bussi, and Patricia V. Agostino, "Minutes, Days and Years: Molecular Interactions Among Different Scales of Biological Timing," *Philosophical Transactions: Biological Sciences* 369, no. 1637, 5 March 2014): 1-12.

added here, one which suggests the sheer diversity of the subject matter. It has dawned gradually over the last decades that a part of the human anatomy that had been disregarded turns out to be vital to the functioning of the human organism: the microorganisms that inhabit the intestinal tract. "Gut bacteria," once thought all but irrelevant to human health turn out via a number of factors to be essential to it. What is doubly surprising is the still more recent discovery is that activities of these bacteria are "timed." That is, they follow the sorts of rhythmic patterns described throughout this chapter, including circadian rhythms.[31] Inversely the rhythmic behavior of gut bacteria then influences the rhythms of the human body *per se*. The optimal result of this elaborate dance (surely a tango) is health. Missteps, flawed orchestrations, produce its opposite.

---

[31] Christopher A. Thaiss, Maayan Levy, and Eran Elinay, "Chronobiomics: The Biological Clock as a New Principle in Host-Microbial Interactions." *PLoS Pathog* 11, no. 10 (8 October 2015): e1005113. https://doi.org/10.1371/journal.ppat.1005113. Also, "Disrupting Gut Bacteria Circadian Rhythm Leads to Serious Health Consequences," *Chronobiology*, https://www.chronobiology.com/disrupting-gut-bacteria-circadian-rhythm-leads-to-serious-health-consequences/. Finally, Scott Anderson, "The Psychobiotic Revolution," *New Scientist* 243, no. 3246 (7 September 2019): 24-28. All articles accessed 24 Jan 2022.

Duration, Neurosis and Dark Time

Up to this point I have dealt with the ways in which Bergson's intuitions have been singled out and developed in memory science, the novel, and biological time. This chapter will look into yet another field to which the philosopher was able to make contributions: psychology. It would be nice if the Bergsonian interactions with psychology were one and simple. They were in fact many and complex. What follows will be an attempt to simplify this complexity by dealing only with the most important of Bergson's speculations. Secondary contributions will be noted in the text or footnotes.

Those major psychologists who seized on important aspects of Bergson's thought are, by my count, four. They are Carl Gustav Jung, Charles Blondel, Pierre Janet, and Eugene Minkowski,. To these will be added Jean Piaget, a name far removed from psychiatry. In this context, I would particularly want to emphasize the work of Eugene Minkowski. Alone among Bergson's appropriators, Minkowski continued to explore the experience of duration, particularly in its relation to mental illness. By concentrating on Minkowski it will be possible to forge a continuity between psychology and what has been written previously on the phenomena of biological time. The human body, as we have seen, exhibits an extraordinary array of temporalities. These have important relations to both our physical and mental health, relations which merit further, detailed investigations.

Minkowski's phenomenological psychology, interesting in itself, makes possible an interrelated study of hour mental illness and biological time.

So: To begin with Jung.

A. Carl Gustav Jung

Perhaps the shortest route in understanding Carl Gustav Jung's relation to Bergson is by looking into Jung's break with his mentor Sigmund Freud. This break--famous in the history of psychoanalysis--had many sources in the personal psychologies and backgrounds of both men. The sticking point, however, was theoretical and involved the concept of libido. For Freud libido, the motive force of human psychology, was purely sexual. Jung seems never to have been convinced by this. Ernst Jones, Freud's biographer, states:

> As early as 1909 Jung was complaining to Freud about his difficulty in explaining to his pupils the concept of libido and begged him for a fuller

definition. Freud tersely replied that he could give no clearer one than he had already. Only two years later Jung equated his version with Bergson's élan vital, with life energy in general, and thus robbed it of its distinctive sexual connotations.[1]

Freud saw Jung's apostasy in the same terms. Writing in 1915 he complained:

> What I have seen of religious-ethical conversions has not been inviting. Jung for example, I found sympathetic so long as he lived blindly, as I did. Then came his religious-ethical crisis with higher morality, "rebirth," Bergson and at the same time lies, brutality, and antisemitic condescension towards me.[2]

That Jung's concepts of libido were virtually identical to Bergson's and strongly influenced by them is undeniable. I have been able to find over a dozen points at which Jung says as much categorically.[3] The driving force of life, if it contains sexuality as one of its components for Jung, cannot for Jung be reduced to sexuality *per se*.

Jung's break with Freud over the concept of libido had two results, one historical the other conceptual. Historically it marked a division within the previously monolithic psychoanalytical movement. The public could now see that capable representatives of that movement could disagree with its founder on central points, not merely on matters of detail. The Jung-Freud split was not to be the last. The psychoanalytic movement has suffered a rhizomatic or ramified fate. In recent editions of *Current Psychotherapies*, R. Corsini and D. Wedding state that there are now over four hundred accepted schools of psychotherapy.[4] It is unlikely that either Freud or Jung would have found this situation satisfactory.

Conceptually the Jung-Freud split resulted in a redefinition of "libido." Jungians argued that this was a shift from a one-sided, dogmatic picture of the forces driving human beings, and was thus beneficial in any number of ways. It enabled a more adequate analysis of the complex structure of human personality, making it possible to more accurately analyze its weaknesses and

---

[1] Ernest Jones, *The Life and Works of Sigmund Freud*, Vol. 2 (London: Hogarth Press, 1955), 143.

[2] Sigmund Freud, "Letter to James Jackson Putnam, July 8, 1915," trans. J. B. Heller, ed. N. G. Hale, Jr., *James Jackson Putnam and Psychoanalysis* (Cambridge, MA: 1971), 188-191.

[3] Pete A. Y. Gunter, "Bergson and Jung," *Journal of the History of Ideas* 43, no. 4 (1982): 635-652. All future references to this item will be cited in the text as BJ.

[4] Raymond Corsini and Danny Wedding, eds., *Current Psychotherapies*, 7th ed. (New York: Thompson, 2005), 527.

divisions.[5] Therapists would, on these grounds not be trapped into believing that neuroses are only derived from sexual conflict when other problems can be the source of the problem. The shift from the Freudian to the Jungian paradigm of the libido was thus to have fundamental theoretical and therapeutic consequences.

Should we give Bergson full credit for this shift? The answer is no. Can we, conversely, give him no credit? The answer is a conditional no. We can argue persuasively that Bergson's divergent concept of evolution, to take only one example, would have helped Jung to rethink the diversity within his "life force." Others of Bergson's contentions would have been useful to Jung in deciding how to conceptualize libido.

The safest thing to say about Bergson's impact on Jung's other ideas is that it was similar to his effect on Jung's concept of the libido or life force: that is, it would have provided positive reinforcement, encouraging him to procede farther on the paths he had already taken. It would also have had effects on many of his ideas: sharpening the definition of some, extending the meanings of others, limiting the extension of others. One would have still had a Jungian psychology, but one which had undergone a kind of "sea change."

Jung gives us ample reason to view his early encounter with Bergson in this way. Writing in 1914 he states:

> ...in my book (*The Psychology of the Unconscious*) the concept of the libido which I have given is parallel to that of the élan vital; my constructive method corresponds to his intuitive method...[6]

He elsewhere adds to the life force and intuition, Bergson's concepts of instinct,[7] the limitations of the human intellect,[8] reaction-formation,[9] introversion-extroversion,[10] and the significance of the present in the genesis of neurosis.[11]

---

[5] Neither Jung nor Freud distanced themselves from the notion of analysis. Freud, as all know, termed his approach psychoanalysis. Jung, not to be outdone, termed his approach analytical psychology.

[6] Carl Gustav Jung, "The Content of the Psychoses, Part II, 1914," trans. M. D. Elder, in *Collected Papers in Analytical Psychology*, ed. C. E. Long. (London: 1922), 351.

[7] Carl Gustav Jung, "Instinct and the Unconscious," in *Contributions to Analytical Psychology*, 247.

[8] "Instinct and the Unconscious," 275.

[9] Carl Gustav Jung, "On Some Crucial Points in Psychoanalysis," in *Collected Papers on Analytical Psychology*, 274-275.

[10] "Crucial Points in Psychoanalysis," 229.

[11] "Crucial Points in Psychoanalysis," 229.

This is a remarkable series of parallels. It covers the major part of both Bergson's and Jung's psychologies. But there are two more components of Jung's thought which were influenced by Bergson, but which Jung had taken from the French psychopathologist, Pierre Janet. Noting that he had studied with Janet in Paris in 1900, Jung states:

> ...he formed my ideas very much. He was a first-class observer, though he had no dynamic psychological theory. It was a sort of physiological theory of unconscious phenomena, the so-called *abaissement du niveau mental*, that is, a certain depotentiation of the tension of consciousness.[12]

The concept of psychological tension in Janet's thought is closely, indeed inescapably, bound up with the concept of "function du real" ("reality function"). The hardest conceivable task, Janet argues, is that of coping with present reality. In a healthy personality psychological tension is maintained and developed and the function of reality is sustained. But when, through an encounter with insuperable obstacles, the tension of personality is broken, we have regression, "*l'abaissement du niveau mental.*" In *Wandlungen II* and in *Psychological Types* (to which we will refer below) Jung continually recurs to these joint notions, reshaping them in terms of his own theory of life energy, directing them against Freud's concept of the self. Janet terms the activity through which the function of reality is made effective through confrontation with reality "presentification." Jung repeatedly returns to this notion, insisting against Freud that mental illness may spring from a failure to deal with present problems, and hence, cannot always be traced to early childhood traumas. Regression, he insists, results in many cases from a fear of present life.

Janet's tandem concepts, "psychological tension" and "function of reality" in one respect certainly derived from his observation of his own patients. (Jung correctly notes that Janet was a first-class observer.) But as elements of theory, they clearly involved Janet's interactions with Bergson. This is affirmed by Bergson himself. In the introduction to the English translation of *Matter and Memory*. Here he notes that these ideas were found "indispensable" by Pierre Janet in the development of "psychasthenic" mental illness (which Jung would later term "introverted schizophrenia"). This idea, which was initially considered paradoxical, has come, Bergson states, to be increasingly accepted by psychologists.[13]

---

[12] Carl Gustav Jung, *C. G. Jung Speaking: Interviews and Encounters*, eds. W. McGuire and R. F. C. Hull (Princeton, NJ: Princeton University Press, 1977), 283.
[13] MM, 15.

It would be nice to end the investigation of the relations between Jung's and Bergson's psychologies here. But Jung was to transform his concepts of intuition and oppose (instead of paralleling) Bergson's. It is worthwhile to examine his new viewpoint. This is presented in *Character Types* (1921).[14]

In *Character Types* Jung outlines four basic human personalities: thinking, feeling, sensational and intuitive. Each of these, he continues, has two alternative modes: introverted and extraverted. There are thus eight character types in all: introverted-thinking, extraverted-thinking, introverted-feeling, etc. Besides the dualism represented by introversion and extraversion there is another profounder dualism at the root of his character types: the cleft between types which are "rational" and those which are "irrational." The first two, thinking and feeling, are described by Jung as rational. Perceiving and intuitive types are, by contrast, categorized as irrational. A great deal hinges on this distinction. What does Jung mean by "irrational"? How does irrationality relate to reason?

In some respects, Jung is quite clear about this distinction. By terming perception and intuition irrational he means simply that

> ...whatever they do or do not do is based not on rational judgment, but on sheer intensity of perception. Their perception is directed simply and solely to events as they happen, no selection being made by judgment.[15]

There is no reason why objects of perception or intuition appear. They are simply raw "givens" for which nothing more can be said. Unfortunately, intuition thus defined turns out to be beyond Bergson's reach. Jung states:

> Bergson, it is true, has drawn attention to the role of intuition and to the possibility of an 'intuitive method.' Any proof of the method is lacking and will not be easy to furnish, notwithstanding Bergson's claim that his '*élan vital*' and '*duree créatrice*' are products of intuition. Aside from these intuitive concepts, which derive their psychological function from the fact that they were current in antiquity, particularly in neoplatonism, Bergson's method is not intuitive but intellectual.[16]

Bergson's presumed intellectualism is thus linked here (with no qualifications) to pragmatism and hence to the philosophy of William James. Jung concludes:

---

[14] Carl Gustav Jung, *Psychological Types* (Princeton: Princeton University Press, 1971), 608. All future references to this work will be cited in the text as CT.

[15] PT, 370.

[16] PT, 320.

James and Bergson are signposts along the road which German philosophy--not of the academic sort--has already trodden.[17]

It is really Nietzsche, the Nietzsche of *Thus Spake Zarathustra*, who is the true intuitionist and the true vanguard of the future.[18]

Jung makes it clear that his rethinking of intuition begins with Nietzsche's distinction in *The Birth of Tragedy* between Apollonian and Dionysiac. Initially these seemed to him fully to describe two fundamental character types: Apollonian as rational and Dionysiac as irrational. Dissatisfied with this simple twofold viewpoint, Jung was to use his interaction with the Zürich Club to help criticize and reshape these ideas. Among the members of this club were Hans Schmidt, Toni Wolff, Emile Medtuer, and Adolf Keller. These were to sharpen and broaden Jung's character typology, breaking down and pluralizing his original two-sided Apollonian-Dionysiac duality.

The realization of Jung's turn toward Nietzsche in *Psychological Types* helps us to understand his new viewpoint. What Bergson lacks, Jung now insists, is Dionysiac inspiration. Lacking a Dionysiac base, Bergson's philosophy is condemned to be unintuitive and merely thinking or concept oriented.

Of the many problems with Jung's new attitude towards Bergson, I will discuss only three: 1. His dismissal of Bergson's duration and *élan vital* as real contributions to psychology. 2. His conflation of Bergson's philosophy with Spinoza's, a conflation which involves 3. A nearly total misunderstanding of the nature of Bergson's method and his concept of intuition.

Jung's treatment of Bergson's duration and élan vital is equivocal. These are, he concedes, archetypes and hence must be structures at the center of his own system. But, given his new devaluing of Bergson's philosophy, he cannot allow the Frenchman credit for them. Jung now insists that intuition and the life force or élan vital cannot be taken seriously as Bergson's contributions, because they appeared already in the philosophy of Plotinus (neoplatonism). But on these grounds, much of Jung's psychology must be declared insignificant, precisely because his theory of archetypes was largely derived from a study of ancient and oriental manuscripts for their archetypal content. Jung's archetypes all had appeared previously in ancient thought.

But are Bergson's notions of duration and the life force merely copies of ancient, much less Plotinian ideas? The answer is that in at least three fundamental respects they are not. Bergson, in *Creative Evolution*, was to draw analogies

---

[17] PT, 321.
[18] PT, 321.

between his philosophy and that of Plotinus. [19] But on at least two points Bergson adds characteristics to the life force which Plotinus rejects. For Plotinus the descent from the world of Platonic forms into the world is a diminution, a falling away from true perfection. Precisely in this respect, his philosophy differs from Plotinus's. The evolution of life is for Bergson an increase of reality, not a diminution. [20] Equally important, for Bergson, biological evolution involves the creation of new forms, new ideas, new values: literally, as I have noted above, new possibilities. One fails to find this idea in classical Greek or Roman philosophy. Equally, the behavior of any life force in ancient thought was understood as an aspect of or as taking place in a cyclical temporality, one repeated *ad infinitum*. This can hardly be said of Bergson's branching temporality, from which any idea of ceaseless repetition must be excluded.

One thus finds in Bergson not a rediscovery of old ideas or archetypes, but a rethinking and reformulation of them. This is true of his philosophy throughout. One never finds in Bergson, what one will in Jung, a desire to reiterate the ancient as a precondition for the Modern. If there is anything like an archetype in Bergson, it requires a reformulation and recreation in order to be real. What life force can one find among the ancients which is thoroughly grounded in the Bergsonian notions of novelty, spontaneity, creativity, and the emergence of the metaphysically new? I am able to find none.

We now come to Jung's equation of the philosophies of Bergson and Spinoza. It is easy to show its weaknesses. For one, Spinoza's philosophy is based on a denial of the reality of time. Bergson's-- the contrast could hardly be more dramatic-- is based on the centrality of time (duration) to any metaphysics or theory of knowledge. Between Spinoza's *sub specie aeternitatus* and Bergson's *sub specie durationis* there is an immense gap. To deal with a second point: Spinoza's philosophy involves the assumption that the philosopher can arrive at absolute certainty -- not only in philosophy but in the sciences as well. Bergson makes no such claim. For him, there remains something contingent in all knowledge, however well founded. Similarly, Spinoza's thought involves a commitment to a metaphysical system, with axioms, definitions, corollaries and theorems assigned their necessary places. Spinoza's masterwork, the *Ethics*, is constructed on the model of geometry: *more geometrica demonstrata*, to use his famous phrase. Bergson's thought is a protest against all such methods with their pretentions of perfect deductive order.

---

[19] CE, 205-207.
[20] CE, 135.

All of these differences become clearer when their implications for philosophical method are examined. Spinoza's universe is, consistently with his method, given all at once: substance, attributes, modes, in descending order. Bergson's method in no way portrays this architectural order. Rather, it resembles a series of ever larger concentric circles, each of which represents an attempt to widen the applications of the idea of duration.[21]

Jung appears not to have understood either the exploratory character of Bergson's philosophy or the notion of intuition which it involves. As I have labored to show throughout this essay, in pursuing method Bergson attempts, by participating in fundamental durations, to discover something of their fundamental character: something which, given our all too human tendency to put things in "freeze frames," we might well have missed. Thus, he was able to make contributions to memory science, the novel, biological time, and psychopathology. A confrontation with Jung at this point helps us to flesh out our understanding of Bergson's notion of intuition, which is:

> ...a concept appropriate to the object alone, a concept one can barely say is still a concept, since it applies to that one thing.[22]

This "unique intuition" or "unique concept"[23] can also be termed a "fluid concept."[24] An intuition, a participation in duration, can then be developed in formal, spatial terms just as a musical idea can be developed into successive sounds and finally is congealed in a music score. That is, to put it simply, an intuition (the musical idea), which begins as a fluid concept can be developed and expressed in terms of briefer durations and finally depicted in spatial form (e.g. the music score). Thus, it is "materialized,"[25] as we will see, the transition from duration to space (e.g. from intuition to analysis), is for Bergson a continuous process descending through contracting levels of duration. It is a transition from intuition to knowledge by ordinary concepts.

For the Jung of *Psychological Types*, however, exactly this transition is forbidden. The knowledge-through perception he equates with the intuitive and sensationalist personality has no conceptual content whatsoever. Since this knowledge is attuned to the absolutely contingent, they "must lack all

---

[21] There are, however, similarities between Bergson's ideas and Spinoza's similarities which Bergson recognized and explored.

[22] CM, 207.

[23] CM, 208.

[24] CM, 207.

[25] Pete A. Y. Gunter, "Bergson, Materialization and the Peculiar Nature of Space" *Lo Sguardo* 1, no. 26, (2018): 231-245.

rational direction."[26] The intuitive person, if he adduces arguments, puts forth arguments which lack "...the convincing power of reason. He can only profess or proclaim. His is the voice of one crying in the wilderness."[27] One can only wonder why he bothers to "cry." He has no concepts of any kind, Jung insists. So no one can know what they are crying about? Jung's limitations of intuition to a state of mind entirely devoid of conceptual content would make communication of any kind impossible for the Nietzschean hero. Yet he would never deny that Nietzsche was able to communicate. Any bridge between intuition in its supposed irrationality and our conceptual thought is forbidden by the Jung of *Psychological Types*. It is present and effective in Bergson.

In an article written in 1913, Jung makes an attempt at forging a bridge (as Bergson would put it) between intuition and analysis, citing William Worringer's concept of aesthetic objects as "crystallizations" of a more fundamental impulse.[28] But Jung, instead of linking this notion to intuition, takes it as an example of intellectual abstraction and clarification[29] and leaves the matter at that.

We come at the end of this confrontation of two fascinating minds to a discovery that might have been presented at the beginning. We have noted Jung's admission that when early on he discovered that the French philosopher had worked out the ideas which he had already formulated. He failed, however, to mention his debt to one idea that Bergson had already worked out, the non-rational character of intuition.[30] Nathalie Pilard notes Jung's admission in a letter (6/14/15) to H. Schmidt-Guisan: "*Von Bergson nämlich bekan' ich der Bergriff des Irrationale.*"[31] That is, "From Bergson I have taken the notion of the irrational."

This admission has two corollaries. It adds to our knowledge of the extent that Bergson's ideas contributed to the development of Jung's thought. But in doing so it exhibits the paradoxical nature of Jung's later response to Bergson. On the one hand, he is able to use Bergson's viewpoint to develop some of his most

---

[26] CT, 455.

[27] CT, 402.

[28] PT, 504.

[29] PT, 504.

[30] Nathalie Pilard, *Jung and Intuition* (London: Karnac, 2015), 301. In many respects, Pilard's book is a study of the relations between Bergson and Jung, particularly pp. 32-37, 156-173.

[31] H. K. Iselin, *Zur Entsehung von C. G. Jungs "Psychologische Typen": Die Briefwchsel zwischen C. G. Jung und Hans Schmidt-Guisan im Lichte ihrer Freundshaft* (Aarou: Saverlander, 1982), 39.

fundamental theories. But, at least in the opinion of this writer, he is unable to do so without making some of his most central ideas unworkable.

B. Charles Blondel

It is hard to imagine two visions of psychopathology more starkly in contrast than those of Carl Gustav Jung and Charles Blondel (1876-1939). While Jung dwells in the plurality of a series of four personality types mediated by introversion and extroversion and a crowded pantheon of archetypes drawn from his voluminous reading, Blondel's psychology is framed in terms of a single simple dualism: the inner self-isolated on one side and the social milieu (Society) on the other. This contrast is nowhere mediated, nowhere attenuated. The two components are at odds and ordinarily irreconcilable. Nothing could be farther from Blondel's grey dualism than Jung's sprawling psychiatric plurality.

Blondel's dualism is inevitable given his acceptance not only of Bergson's first-person psychology[32] but of the emphatically third-person sociology of Emile Durkheim. For Durkheim the social fabric is not only the sole determinant of human thought and behavior: it is all that exists. The individual person, so central to Bergson's philosophy, is for Durkheim's sociology only a temporary thread in the social fabric.

Ordinarily, the social person, fitting in with the norms of its society, functions effectively. Mental illness, Blondel argues, arises when the personal and the social cease to function together. In the words of Joseph Parnas:

> ...when certain prereflective affections surpassed the subject's capacity for a socially adequate linguistic communicative discharge, a psychiatric symptom was formulated through a highly subjective conceptualization.[33]

This conflict between the "inner" and the "social" self has fascinating implications for the use of language. When the mentally ill person tries to express their response to their situation, they are attempting to articulate a purely personal, purely subjective state in a socially constructed language. In spite of the fact that they are using ordinary words and syntax, they cannot communicate. Each is speaking a private language.

---

[32] Henri Wallon, "The Psychological and Sociological Study of the Child," in *The World of Henri Wallon*, trans. D. Nicholson Smith.

[33] Josef Parnas, "Introduction to History and Epistemology of Psychopathology," in *Philosophical Issues in Psychiatry*, eds. K. S. Kendler and J. Parnas (Oxford: Oxford University Press, 2015), 28.

A difficult effort of translation would be necessary to understand the pathological language ("*language morbide*") of the mentally ill.[34] We can only hope to understand the symptoms of which the neurotic complains. In the patient's mind,[35] pathological symptoms, physical (*corporeal*) negations, organic and affective insensibility, moral and physical suffering interpenetrate in strange, unfamiliar ways. It is impossible to find logical organization:

> ...in the patient's speech of a delerious patient or any of the methodological moves of discursive thought. One finds (instead) a polymorphism, a multiplicity of morbid orientations of all degrees...The systematization of the delirium of our patients escape, therefore, our logic.[36]

What we find in the neurotic are systemizations which are not logical but living and felt.[37]

It is easy to find the source of Blondel's psychological and linguistic dualisms in *Time and Free Will*. In this work, as we have sketched earlier, he discovers a sharp gap between the dynamic, continuous duration of the inner self and the static discontinuity of space: clock time. Bergson insists that this contrast is accompanied by a linguistic dualism. The idea of our inner life "...cannot be translated into the language of common sense."[38] The deep-seated self,

> which heats and blazes up, is a self whose states and changes permeate one another and undergo a deep alteration, (but) as we separate them from one antoher (we) set them out in space.[39]

Thus, refracted and broken into pieces, the self...

> is much better adapted to the requirements of social life in general *and language in particular*. Consciousness prefers it and gradually loses sight of the fundamental self.[40]

Clearly, Blondel uses exactly these distinctions in separating the inner self from both the social world of the embodied human being and the socially-constituted

---

[34] Charles A. A. Blondel, *La Conscience Morbide: Essai de Psychopathologie Generale* (Paris: Felix Alcan, 1914), 163. Published by Wentworth Press, an imprint of Creative Media Partners. (All future references to this work will be cited in the text as LCM.) All translations of Blondel's text into English are those of the author.

[35] So to speak.

[36] LCM, 210.

[37] LCM, 210.

[38] TFW, 122.

[39] TFW, 125.

[40] TFW, 129. Emphasis mine.

language that mentally ill persons on his terms are condemned to use. It is hardly accidental that the concluding pages of *La Conscience Morbide* are devoted to a discussion of the contrast between the dynamics of inner duration and the static character of homogeneous space.[41]

The Bergson of *Time and Free Will* and the Blondel of *La Conscience Morbide* agree in proposing the strict contrast between the personal and the social and the accompanying dichotomy of duration and space. They diverge profoundly, however, in their accounts of the relations between the two realms. For Bergson, as we have seen, the free act is not imprisoned in a subjective duration. Bergson clearly intends that it expresses itself in the world, in acts. The possibility of such physically expressed freedom is not explained in *Time and Free Will*. But the transition between inner duration and biological duration that he describes in *Matter and Memory* makes intelligible the physical embodiment of the free act. For him the inner can impact the "outer." Not so for Blondel.

It is hard to sum up the significance of Blondel's psychopathology. It is also, and partly for this reason, difficult to evaluate Bergson's full contribution to Blondel's thought. Jose M. Villagran states that *La Conscience Morbide* is one of the five most important ("seminal") books written in the history of psychotherapy.[42] A similar opinion is offered by Henri Wallon,[43] who notes the novelty of a number of Blondel's theses later adopted by others.

We seem to find in Blondel a lone figure, to whom many have turned for insights and examples, but who can never be said to have started a movement or founded a school of psychopathology. The reason is not far to seek. In Blondel there are striking case histories, brilliant conceptual studies, and an emphasis on factors neglected by many psychotherapists. What there does not appear to be an account of any means of alleviating the suffering of the mentally ill. This--a <u>cure</u>--appears to be entirely lacking in his writings. His dramatic dualism, resolutely and capably defended, portrays a conflict to

---

[41] LCM, 315-335.

[42] Jose M. Villagran, "Consciousness Disorders in Schizophrenia: A Forgotten Land for Psychopathology," *International Journal of Psychology and Psychological Theory* 3, no. 2 (2003): 216. The same claims are made by F. Fuentenebra and G.E. Berrios, "Charles Blondel and *La Conscience Morbide*," in *History of Psychiatry*, Vol. VIII (1997), 277. Berrios adds that Blondel is "arguably the most original writer (and less known to English-speaking mental health workers) in the field." G.E. Berrios, *History of Mental Symptoms: Descriptive Psychopathology Since the Nineteenth Century* (Cambridge: Cambridge University Press, 1996), 120-121.

[43] Henri Wallon, "Une Psychologie Humaniste: Charles Blondel," in *Enfance*, Vol. 21, no. 1-2 (1968), 103-109.

which he finds no resolution. Like the later Freud, he can be said to have developed a therapeutic pessimism.[44]

One final point should be added here. This concerns Blondel's portrayal of the mentally ill.[45] One may criticize his treatment of the language of the mental patient as an entirely private language (or on some interpretations as no language at all). The fact remains that one of Blondel's major contributions is to have drawn attention to the nature of this language and the difficulties involved in trying to understand it.

C. Eugene Minkowski

Though Jung and Blondel, in their quite different ways, were able to use Bergson's ideas to explore and deepen their concepts of mental illness, in doing so neither concentrated on the concept of duration. The opposite is true of Eugene Minkowski who in utilizing Bergson's views, puts duration center stage. From Minkowski's viewpoint to explore duration is to discover the fundamental conditions for mental illness. To fail to do so is to overlook the significance of basic attitudes towards time and the conditions which they generate.

Born in Saint Petersburg, Minkowski (1885-1972) was to emigrate to Switzerland where he worked at the famous Burgholzi clinic. He then established himself in Paris.[46] Like Blondel, though without the complexities engendered by Blondel's joint alliance with Durkheim, he was an avowed follower of Bergson. He was more, however, than a follower. He was, with W. L. Binswanger, a founder of phenomenological psychiatry.

What one sees in Minkowski is the careful application of Bergson's basic ideas concerning duration, memory, and perception to the problems of psychopathology. The end result of this carry-over, this development from intuition to a renewed and enlarged analysis, is a singling out of temporal structures. Minkowski as a rule calls them "organizing structures" through which we regulate our behavior and maintain our sense of self.

---

[44] For criticisms of Blondel's sociological psychology, see Sylvain de Coster, "In Memoriam La psychologie sociologique de Charles Blondel," in *Revue Internationale de Psychologie* 1, no. 3 (1939), esp. 578-579.

[45] For an English translation of a chapter in *La Conscience Morbide* devoted to the problem of language, see Charles Blondel, "Insane Thought and Language," in *The Troubled Conscience and the Insane Mind*, trans. F.G. Crookshank (London: Kegan Paul Trench Trübner & Co., 1928), 68-91. Reprinted London: Routledge, 2014

[46] For a fuller account of Minkowski's transits from Russia to Poland to Switzerland to France, see D.F. Aller and J. Postel, "Eugeniusz Minkowski ou une vision de la schizophrénie," in *L'évolution psychiatrique* 60, no. 4 (1995): 161-196.

The relevance of these temporal structures is made clear by Rollo May. The essence of depression, he states in a discussion of Minkowski, is the slowing down and virtual cessation of duration. The future is blocked; the past can no longer be brought to bear on the present. As with the manic patient the depressed patient lives in a false present. In the case of the "manic" patient, this stasis of blockage is veiled. In the depressive, it is starkly present. Reflecting on his experience with depressive patients, Rollo May states:

> ...if we can help the severely anxious or depressed patient to focus on some point in the future when he will be outside his anxiety or depression, the battle is half won. Focusing upon some point in time outside the depression of anxiety gives his patient a perspective, a view from on high.[47]

This may in turn break the chains of depression with its diminished, retarded time and provide the beginnings of a way out.

Underlying this description of depression there is a hidden assumption: that causal order in the life of the mind always proceeds from past through present with the distant past dominating the present. But something entirely different can take place. Minkowski believes that mental illness can arise in our later lives, generated by newly accumulated negative factors. These in turn can reactivate negative factors in the past and make them active in the present. If a serious error is made or a wrong act committed, these can by themselves generate persisting negative symptoms, which become engraved in our memories. These in turn can cloud our vision of the future and, effectively, close it off for us. Time (that is, our inner duration), slows. The word seems strange and distant.

We thus begin to lose the possibility of performing positive acts in the future. The capacity to compensate for our failures or our transgressions, Minkowski states, is an ordinary factor in our lives. He states:

> ...the unique meaning of positive results produced or good acts resides in the fact that we can do better, in the future. Our whole personal evolution consists in the desire to surpass works already accomplished. But where our mental life dims, the future closes before us. At the same time, the idea of positive results in the past, which is a function of the past, disappears. The memory remains intact but it is the static notion

---

[47] Rollo May, *The Discovery of Being: Writings in Existential Psychology* (New York: W.W. Norton and Company, 1983), 135.

of evil which predominates. Our patient will say that he is the worst patient in the world, and will see concretized remorse everywhere.[48]

In both schizophrenia and bipolar disorder, the patient is cut off from the future. In that future he or she might expiate bad actions by doing good ones.[49] Absence of the common feeling of accomplishment and of the connectedness of ones acts[50] can be understood to generate guilt, compensatory hallucinations, and poisonous self-doubt.

This is the polar opposite of Freud's position. For him, it is always the much earlier (and presumably traumatic) experience that explains the later neurosis. By contrast, Minkowski explains mental illness, not in terms of Freud's "chronologic," but on the assumption that it is the most essential aspects of experience, *earlier or later*, that are the "ground" of our personality.[51] To reiterate the point: the earlier parts of the patient's experience, assumed to be the real, determining causes of mental illness, may only become significant when entrained by and made part of problems that emerge later--perhaps much later.

That psychological problems are rooted in disorders of basic temporality is supported by another set of Minkowski's discoveries. A patient reports:

> Time is immobile. You hesitate between the past and the future. Everything is so rooted. Before there was a before and an after. Yet it isn't there now. It is a boring time, drawn out without end, and I can no longer do anything.[52]

Another laments that each day is a separate island.[53] Another complains that he desires to remain exactly as he is, immune from change.[54] The future is blocked.[55]

Still another symptom of mental illness is a tendency toward "morbid geometrism" or "morbid rationalism." Minkowski, like Bergson, has nothing against either the use of geometry or the employment of the human intellect.

---

[48] Eugene Minkowski, *Lived Time*, trans. Nancy Metzel (Evanston, IL: Northwestern University Press, 1970), 193. All future references to this work will be cited in the text as LT.

[49] LT, 347.

[50] LT, 331.

[51] Stephen Kern, "Time and Medicine," *Annals of Internal Medicine* 132, no.1 (2000): 3-8.

[52] LT, 286.

[53] LT, 186.

[54] LT, 235.

[55] LT, 187.

There is nothing "sick" about either. But this capacity can become deformed. A banal example is a patient who informed Minkowski that the enlarging of a railroad station (a spatial event) is far more important than the state (the "fluctuation") of the national economy (certainly a temporal process).[56] More bizarre is the case of the patient who replaces the world around him with geometrical figures:

> What upsets me a lot is that I have a tendency to see only the skeleton of things. I see people as points or circles. When I think of a meeting I must attend, I see the room. I see the people present as points.[57]

Similarly, Louis A. Sass describes a patient asked to draw a picture of her family. The patient obliged, drawing a large circle surrounded by four or five small circles. This, he said, was his family sitting around the kitchen table.[58]

Morbid rationalism, as the example just given suggests, is closely related to morbid geometrism. In the normal person the search for theory, for abstract principles, is constrained by the intuitive grasp of context and thus a sense of limits. For morbid rationalists, there is none of this. Their thinking consists of an endless, often aimless search for abstract concepts. One, Minkowski notes,

> ...adopts (a particular) pedagogical system, changing its principle once a week: he changes between strict military discipline to a principle of absolute indulgence or a liberal principle of tenderness.' His utterances are determined by the chosen principle, which means that most of the time he does not speak at all.[59]

The connections between such a standpoint and either the content of his course or the student taking it is nowhere to be found. The schizoid over-rationalizes and over-thinks, endlessly reexamining the facts, but without an effort to resolve actual problems.

Perhaps it will help to restate our description of Minkowski's psychotherapy. For Bergson, our lives are lived in an oscillating present. Bored or interested, sleepy or focused, for the normal person the durations associated with these states vary within fairly well-established limits. Minkowski accepts this description of normal psychology. But he expands Bergson's ideas into abnormal psychology,

---

[56] LT, 116.

[57] Eugene Minkowski, *Traite de psychopathologie* (Paris: Institut Synthelabo, 1999), 326f.

[58] Louis A. Sass, "Self and World in Schizophrenia," *Philosophy, Psychiatry, and Psychology* 8, no.4 (2001): 258.

[59] Eugene Minkowski, *Au-delà du rationalisme morbide* (Paris: Ed. L'Harmattan, 1997), 51-58.

which Bergson deals within his writings but does not concentrate on. Here Minkowski finds a constant in the mindset of his patients. That is, often in spite of appearances [60] the mentally ill find themselves caught in an inflexible enfeebling temporality characterized by repetition. Their lives are thus caught in the lower levels of Bergson's temporal hierarchy, where repetition and pronounced spatiality reign. Unsurprisingly, they inform the psychotherapist of their boredom and alienation and of the "strangeness" of the world.

This painful descent down the temporal staircase is the basis, Minkowski finds, for all forms of mental illness. If the patient is introverted, Minkowski terms their illness schizophrenic; if extroverted, syntonic. [61] Either set of illnesses is bound to fundamental inability to bring their experience and their fundamental beliefs into their lives. In this sense their problem stems from an inability to act. This in turn follows from the derailment of their lives into a subterranean world of repetition and psychological paralysis. The psychiatrist's goal, if this is true, is to find the sources of this derailment and bring the future back to life. [62]

D. Pierre Janet

In writing a section of articles on Bergson and psychology, I had hoped to discuss Bergson's contemporary, Pierre Janet in depth. One would think that this would be easy to do. After all, the two were personal friends, colleagues at the Collège de France, and in personal communication throughout their lives. [63] Surely there are numerous personal accounts of their communications, scientific, philosophical and personal. There ought also to be a fund of letters and other exchanges that help us to see the sources and interrelations of their ideas. None of this exists, not a scrap. Or at least not a scrap that this writer can find.

It is clear that Bergson's thinking was influenced by Janet's. In *Matter and Memory*, he cites three of his colleague's books. In chronological order they are *Automatisme psychologique* (1889), *État mental des hysteriques* (1894), and *Les*

---

[60] For example, the manic may seem extremely vital and active. But this is a pantomime tied to an underlying dullness and lack.

[61] This would involve, particularly, the extraverts. Syntony means, for Minkowski, the capacity to "vibrate" in unison with the environment.

[62] Pete A.Y. Gunter, "Bergson's Divided Line and Minkowski's Psychiatry: The Way Down," in *Chromatikon IV* (Louvain: Presses Universitaires de Louvain, 2008), 107-119.

[63] On my last visit to Paris, I was told that the Bergsons and the Janets babysat each other's children. This would be taken almost anywhere as an example of a close relationship, both familial and personal.

Obsessions et la psychothénie (1903).[64] Henri Ellenberger notes that he utilized one of Janet's terms, "*function fabulatrice.*"[65] As for the Bergsonian concepts that Janet was able to take over and utilize, there are two (which we have already noted with regard to Carl Gustav Jung). These are cited by Bergson in his introduction to the English translation of *Matter and Memory*. Here he proclaims the concept of "attention to life" as the starting point of his research into memory and the levels of human consciousness.[66] On the next page he cites "psychic tension" as a fundamental idea closely linked to "attention to life."[67] He then footnotes Janet's *Les Obsessions et la psychothénie* as a study that has been able successfully to employ these ideas. Janet never objected to Bergson's treatment of his work, with its claim of priority. I am also glad to have the agreement of Henri Ellenberger, the historian of dynamic psychiatry, who also notes Janet's admission that Bergson's thought played a significant role in formulating his later treatment of psychological facts as "conducts" (i.e. his later "social behaviorism").[68]

So far it has been possible to show that Bergson's thought had a significant impact on four major psychologists: Jung, Blondel, Minkowski and Janet. But his influence was not limited to psychiatry. It extended to parts of psychology far removed from questions of the unconscious and mental illness. Among the most significant of these is genetic epistemology, a theory of learning developed by the Swiss psychologist Jean Piaget. But, as we will see, there are others. I will deal with them after discussing Bergson's impact on Piaget.

E. Jean Piaget

A prodigy, by the time he was ten, Piaget had begun publishing articles on the mollusks of Switzerland. As a teenager, he was even offered a position in a scientific institution on the basis of his articles (The offer was rescinded when his age became known). The young author seemed headed for an orthodox scientific career in biology but an encounter with philosophy was to change that. Samuel Cornut, Piaget's godfather, believed that Piaget's concentration on a single technical field was narrowing his mind, making him overspecialized.

---

[64] MM, 251, 255.

[65] Henri Ellenberger, *The Discovery of the Unconscious* (New York: Basic Books, 1970), 345. (All future references to this work will be cited in the text as DU.)

[66] MM, 14.

[67] MM, 15

[68] DU, 354-355.

He introduced Piaget to *L'évolution créatice.*[69] The result was, for a time, the young man's total conversion to Bergson's philosophy. He was to give talks to a group of young naturalists on the failure of biological taxonomy (classification)[70] and the flaws of Mendelian genetics.[71]

The problem was that Piaget hoped to find in Bergson a science heavily factual and equipped with accurate formulas. This was something Bergson did not attempt to do. Rather, it is almost the entire argument of this book he attempted to arrive at conclusions that feed into the sciences and help create new sciences. But the philosopher, he thought, should not attempt to pose as a scientist. Piaget turned elsewhere, seeking ideas that would lead to scientific conceptualizations.

The result was paradoxical. Though he never ceased criticizing Bergson's philosophy[72] and though he considered his exposure to Bergson's' ideas "unfortunate,"[73] it was through this exposure that Piaget obtained the ideas which formed the basis for his life's research.

What did Bergson say that led Piaget into his successful research? To put it very simply, that theory of life and theory of knowledge are one.[74] That is, human thinking and human conceptual schemes are not simply given, in the nature of things they are the creations of a particular kind of organism forced to cope in order to survive. They are the result of a constant interaction of the organism and the world. This interactive concept of knowledge follows from both Bergson's biology and his psychology. It is summed up in the term adaptation.

It is true, Bergson concedes, that organisms, in order to survive and continue to evolve, must adapt to their environment. Adaptation, however, is not a simple fitting to environmental factors. It consists of the creation of structures which are not simple copies of the environmental features which they utilize.

---

[69] Dominic J. Balestra, "The Mind of Jean Piaget: Its Philosophical Roots," *Thought* 55, no. 210 (1988): 412-427.

[70] Fernando Vidal, *"La vanité de la nomenclature:* Un manuscrit inédit de Jean Piaget," *History and Philosophy of the Life Sciences* 6, no.1 (1984): 75-106.

[71] Fernando Vidal, "Jean Piaget's Early Critique of Mendelism: La notion de l'espèce suivant l'ecole mendélienne," *History and Philosophy of the Life Sciences* 14, no.1 (1992): 113-115.

[72] Laurent Fedi, "Un cas de reception: Piaget lecture de *L'évolution créatice,"* in *Les Annales Bergsoniennes IV* (Paris: Presses Universitaires de France, 2008), 237-254.

[73] Jean Piaget, "Autobiographical note," in *A History of Psychology in Autobiography,* eds. E. Boring et al. (New York: Russell and Russell, 1952), 237-256, esp. 241.

[74] CE, xxxvii.

The eye deals effectively with light, but in no way resembles a set of photons. What is true of an organ (or for that matter of an organism) is true of knowledge. It must be created *en route*. It is a positive or creative adaptation[75] always in the process of being attained. In the words of Dominc J. Balestra,

> ...notions of a non-mechanistic form of evolution which would allow genuine novelty without losing connection with the past, its talk of organisms, species, and adaptation, an above all its theme of the human intellect as an instrument of as well as an instance of evolutionary adaptation have become and still remain essential ingredients in Piaget's theory.[76]

Piaget, Balestra continues, develops a terminology for describing conceptual growth, a terminology he retains throughout his career. Adaptation and equilibrium are the most fundamental.

Adaptation involves the child's changing to meet its situational demands. It operates differently at each developmental stage, yet at each stage utilizes the same two operations: assimilation and accommodation. As an assimilator, the child applies prior concepts to new phenomena (new to the child). Accommodating, by contrast, is the altering of previous concepts in the face of new information.

Equilibrium is the result of successful adaptation. It is a successful balance between the child's capacities and the demands of their situation. Stable in itself, it makes it possible for the child to continue moving along its developmental pathways toward the net higher stage. Piaget views these developmental pathways as a series of increasingly elevated plateaus leading to the highest promontory, adulthood. The plateaus (periods of active inner-outer stability) have four stages: sensorimotor (ages 0-2); proportional (ages 2-7); concrete operations (ages 7-11); and formal operations (ages 12+). The sensorimotor stage exhibits the child's exploration of its body and close environment: the stage of the education of the senses. The fourth stage, formal operations, exhibits the capacity for abstract thought and for dealing objectively with the world.

Piaget's genetic psychology has been widely criticized. It lacks attention to the emotional side of the child and to a multiplicity of perceptual factors which he

---

[75] CE, 37-28; 66-69.

[76] Dominic J. Balestra, "The Mind of Jean Piaget: Its Philosophic Roots," *Thought* 55, no. 219 (1980): 415. An identical view of the relations between Bergson and Piaget, stressing their common commitment to the primacy of action is given by Robert S. Brumbaugh and Nathaniel M. Lawrence, *Philosophical Themes in Modern Education* (Boston: Haughton Mifflin, 1973), 212-215, 235.

never considered. Equally, his notion of distance and time are questioned by experimental psychology.[77] But Piaget was the first to make a systematic study of the child's cognitive development. Prior to his work, it was assumed that the child possesses all the conceptual capabilities of the adult but in diminished degree. Piaget proved that the child thinks not less than adults but differently. He was able to make a good case for explaining the steps in the process.

In at least two respects it is interesting to reflect on the chance meeting of Bergson and the young Piaget. The first involves his rejection of psychological time, which he regarded, alternatively, as a "mistake" or an "illusion." This is particularly strange when we realize that the biological theory of knowledge which in a broad sense he shares with the French philosopher (and many others (Hans Reichenbach and Karl Popper among them,)[78] involves as its components in temporality both biological and psychological. The mind of a child on Piaget's terms goes through a process of creative emergence moving continuously through successive stages, each of which ushers in the next. If this is not a psychological duration, what is?

In spite of Piaget's differences with Bergson, it is clear that this is not the whole story. It would not have been inconsistent for the Swiss theorist of knowledge to deny many of Bergson's ideas and formulate alternative ideas to take their place while still retaining one basic and central idea taken from Bergson: that knowledge and its components fundamentally develop; they are not the result of a set of categories present when knowing begins. Piaget admitted as much. As a young professor, we learn, he went to Paris to hear Bergson speak.[79] Bergson's lecture, he states, helped give him an idea of how to proceed in his research. Furthermore, as Milič Čapek notes, in 1959, Piaget published a letter in the *Revue Théologie et de Philosophie* wherein he states that it was his reading of *Creative Evolution* which gave him the idea of a biological and genetic theory of knowledge.[80]

---

[77] Matthew Edlund, *Psychological Time and Mental Illness* (New York: Gardner Press, Inc., 1987), 5, 48-51.

[78] Milič Čapek, "The Philosophical Significance of Piaget's Researches on the Genesis of the Concept of Time," in *Naturalistic Epistemology*, eds. A. Shimony and D. Nails (Dordrecht-Holland: D. Reidel, 1987), 91-118.

[79] "Jean Piaget," 2022. Website: https://www.bartleby.com/essay/Jean-Piaget-PK4HA4YVC. Accessed 18 Feb 2022.

[80] Jean Piaget, Letter, *Revue de Théologie et Philosophie* (IX, 1959), 44.

F. Other Influences: A Long (and Incomplete) List

The question of Bergson's impact on psychology engages far beyond the five figures outlined above. It involves many others and, as the case of Jean Piaget suggests, these range far beyond the confines of psychiatry.[81] The list could be longer than I have made it. Its very incompleteness, however, comes with a plea for a truly systematic study of the relations between Bergson's' thought and the many components of psychology. Perhaps the concession that the list could be much longer and could be presented in greater detail will lead others to make a more complete study.[82]

These psychologists who have been able to utilize Bergson includes a fifth psychiatrist, Alfred Adler. Paul Schrecker, an Adlerian, employed Bergson to deal with the significance of early childhood memories.[83] Schrecker notes that Adler utilized Bergson's studies of memory to develop his system of dynamic psychiatry.[84] Similarly, the American psychiatrists Harry Stack Sullivan and Wilfred Bion were able to appropriate Bergson's ideas, Sullivan to help define his concept of sympathy[85] and Bion (who also utilized the ideas of A. N. Whitehead) to develop his general system.[86]

One can add to these psychologists the psychotherapists influenced by the work of Eugene Minkowski. Among these (and to this author's surprise) is the anti-psychoanalytic psychotherapist Ronald D. Laing, who credited Minkowski with being the first in the history of psychiatry "to have made a serious attempt

---

[81] Bergson's studies of dreams and laughter and his place in the thought of those whose work straddles the borders between philosophy and psychology (Max Scheler and Maurice Merleau-Ponty for example) have been excluded, as have figures like James Jackson Putnam, who used Bergson's philosophy to introduce Freud to America.

[82] A study of this kind has been undertaken exploring Bergson's influence on biology in Emily Hering, "Henri Bergson's *Creative Evolution* and 20th Century British Biology," PhD Thesis (Leeds: University of Leeds, May 2020).

[83] Paul Schrecker, "Individual Psychological Significance of First Childhood Recollections," *Journal of Individual Psychology* 29, no. 2 (1973): 146-156.

[84] Schrecker, 146-156.

[85] Dieter Wyss, *Psychoanalytic Schools from the Beginning to the Present*, trans. G. Onn (New York: Jason Aronson, Inc., 1973), 282. On this factor, also Max Scheler, *The Nature of Sympathy*, trans. P. Heath (London: Routledge and Kegan Paul, 1954), 364.

[86] Nuno Torres, "Intuition and Ultimate Reality in Psychoanalysis: Bion's Implicit Use of Bergson's and Whitehead's Notions," in *Bion's Sources*, eds. N. Torres and R. D. Hinshelwood (New York: Routledge, 2013), 20-34.

to reconstruct the lived experience of the other."[87] Others who followed Minkowski's lead include academics associated with the journal *Évolution psychiatrique*, for example, Henri Ey and Georges Lanteri-Laura.[88]

Among those psychoanalysts who approached Bergson's philosophy of duration from the viewpoint of biology are Raoul Mourgue and Constantin von Monakow.[89] Along with his laboratory studies on the structure of the brain, von Monakow developed a "hormic" concept of brain function and of human creativity which he allied with Bergson's philosophy.[90] Mourgue was both an avowed disciple of the French intuitionist and extended Bergson's ideas in terms of problems of hallucination.[91]

The remainder of this catalogue is a catch-all, consisting of significantly contrasting thinkers. The British psychologist William McDougall presented experimental evidence to support Bergson's distinction between habitual memory and spontaneous (epochal) memory.[92] The Danish-Icelandic thinker Guðmundur Finnbogason, like Harry Stack Sullivan, used Bergson's intuition to develop a concept of sympathy.[93] Alfred Schutz employed a mixture of ideas from Bergson and Edmund Husserl to create a stronger foundation for the sociology of Max Weber, thus bringing a broadly phenomenological view into the study of sociology.[94] Three other sources important for any study of

---

[87] Ronal D. Laing, "Minkowski and Schizophrenia," *Review of Existential Psychology and Psychiatry* 9 (1963): 195-207. Also, D. F. Allen and J. Postel, "Eugeniusz Minkowski ou une vision de la schizophrénie," *L'Evolution psychiatrique* 60, no.4 (1995): 961-968.

[88] "Obituary: Georges Lanteri-Laura." *History of Psychiatry* 16, no. 3 (2005): 365-372.

[89] Raoul Mourgue and Constantin von Monakow. *Introduction biologique a l'étude de la Neurologie et de la Psychopathologie* (Paris: Alcan, 1928), xi, 120.

[90] Constantin von Monakow, *Emotions, Morality, and the Brain* (Washington: Nervous and Mental Disease Publishing, 1925), 95. (Nervous and Mental Disease Monograph Series, No. 39.)

[91] Raoul Mourgue, *Neurobiologie de l'hallucination. Essai d'une variété particulière de désintégration de la fonction.* Pref. H. Bergson (Brussels: Maurice Lamerton, 1932), 416.

[92] William McDougall and Mary Smith, "Some Experiments in Learning and Attention," *British Journal of Psychology*, 10 no. 2-3 (1919-1920): 199-209.

[93] J. L. Pind, "Guðmundur Finnbogason: 'Sympathetic Understanding' and early Icelandic psychology," *History of Psychology* 11, no. 2 (2008): 75-100. Also, G. Finnbogason. *L'Intelligence sympathétique*, trans. André Courmont (Paris: Félix Alcan, 1913), 244.

[94] Alfred Schutz, *Life Forms and Meaning Structure* (New York: Routledge, 2014), 232. Also, H. R. Wagner, *A Bergsonian Bridge to Phenomenological Psychology* (Lanham, MD: University Press of America, 1984), 184. Finally, Lenore Langsdorf, "Schutz's Bergsonian Analysis of the Structure of Consciousness" *Human Studies* 8, no. 4 (1985): 316-324.

Bergson and psychology Albert Spaier[95], Désiré Roustan[96], and Georges Dwelshauvers.[97]

Finally, since this section began with an account of Bergson's impact on the thought of Carl Gustav Jung, it seems only fitting to end it with a referent to a thinker who deserves to be better known, Beatrice Hinkle. An American psychiatrist who took the lead in bringing Jung's ideas to the United States and in showing the extent to which Jung's and Bergson's psychologies were closely similar.

Hinkle, who began her studies with Sigmund Freud, parted with the Founder of psychoanalysis over his view of women's personality as secondary to and a sort of pale copy of male psychology. Jung took the opposite view: that the child's relation to the mother is the determining factor in its development.

Hinkle's viewpoint is presented in an article in the 1914 *New York Medical Journal*: "Jung's Libido Theory and the Bergsonian Philosophy."[98] Here Hinkle, not surprisingly, bases her views on Jung's reformation of Freud's omnisexual libido to include drives which are equally powerful in human development, but which cannot be reduced genital sex.[99] Like Jung, Janet and many non-Freudians, she traces the origins of neurosis not to the traumas of early childhood but on problems in the present: what duties or tasks is the patient avoiding or what obstacles in his past is he or she trying to overcome? She provides three cases for study: a paralytic; a bedridden neurotic; and a patient complaining of nausea, headaches, and a fear of her acquaintances.[100] All three are women, a point that is worth stressing. Hinkle was a leader in the early feminist movement in the United States. Her Bergsonian-Jungian standpoint clearly had a strong influence on her psychiatry, and vice versa.[101]

---

[95] Albert Spaier, *La pensée concrète* (Paris: Alcan, 1927), 446.

[96] Désiré Roustan, *Psychologie* (Paris: Delagrave, 1911), 510.

[97] Georges Dwelshauvers, *Traité de psychologie* (Paris: Payot, 1934), 606.

[98] Beatrice Hinkle, "Jung's Libido Theory and the Bergsonian Philosophy," *New York Medical Journal* 30 (1914): 1080-1086. All future references to this work will be cited in the text as JLT.

[99] JLT, 1081.

[100] JLT, 1082-1086.

[101] Kate Wittenstein, "The Feminist Uses of Psychoanalysis: Beatrice Hinkle and the Foreshadowing of Modern feminism in the United States," *Journal of Women's History* 10, no. 2 (1998): 38-62.

One finds the same viewpoint in *Recreating the Individual* (1923) in which the Jungian and Bergsonian concept of the libido is stressed.[102] The introduction of this work contains a quote form Bergson.[103] One thus sees in Hinkle a positive and constructive impact of his thought and his approach to thinking. His philosophy, once understood, could help engender ideas as well as be a vehicle for their dissemination.

G. Some Speculations on Duration and Cyclical Addiction

The first sections of this essay present a classical philosophical problem: the mind-body dualism. As we have seen, mind and body are understood by Descartes to be two radically different sorts of substance. On such grounds it is impossible to-see how they could ever interact. Bergson, by contrast, describes both mind and body, mind and organism as comprised of rhythms of duration. If this is so, then the human stream of consciousness and the biological processes of the living organism are both rhythms of duration. I have argued that this fact is far from a dead end. It is an opening into any number of fruitful investigations operating, as I have tried to show, on multiple levels. Equally important is the potential of this durational viewpoint for shedding light on the mind-body problem. That is, if mind and body are both comprised of rhythms of duration; surely it is possible for them to interrelate and interact. One can at least begin to see how this is possible.

Minkowski's researches are not only a classic example of how the study of Bergson can lead to a more detailed (more analytic) account of the way in which duration is structured, both in normal life and mental illness. Through Minkowski Bergson's philosophy is thereby brought nearer to the varieties of experience and, to the capacity to single out the types of psychological pathology.

The difficulty, at least for this writer, is that these valuable researches and the compendium of Minkowski's bright insights remain suspended in midair. We live with and in a living body. If, as I have continually stressed, this body consists of rhythms of duration at every level, the question immediately arises of how the pulsed, rhythmic stream of consciousness relates to the many, profoundly organized durations of the human body. There is no question but what such relations exist. One only has to note the bodily rhythms orchestrated by the brain's suprachasmiatic nucleus. Sleep rhythms, body temperature

---

[102] Beatrice Hinkle, *Recreating the Individual: Study of Psychological Types and Their Relation to Psychoanalysis* (London: George Allen & Unwin, 1923), 23.

[103] Jay Sherry, "Beatrice Hinkle and the Early History of Jungian Psychology in New York," *Behavioral Science* 2, no. 3 (2013): 492-500. I would like to thank Dr. Sherry for bringing Beatrice Hinkle to my attention.

rhythms, heart rhythms are kept in synch by this magisterial conductor. But quite obviously our state of mind is affected by these bodily rhythms. One only needs to think of the effects of an interruption of the sleep cycle. This is well known in jet lag or shift work which interrupt and destabilize the sleep cycle. All of us have felt the psychological effects of being unable to sleep.[104]

Bodily temporality is not limited to the 11,000 cells of the suprachiasmtic nucleus. As I have pointed out, every cell in the body--a relatively recent discovery--has a temporality of its own: its own unique rhythmic structure. The brain merely orchestrates these. In this sense, it is a *Zeitgeber*. But, to repeat the point, it does not give cells their temporality. Their temporality is part of their original nature.

It is clear, at least to this writer, that Minkowski's phenomenological-psychopathology needs to be supplemented by and interrelated with an account of bodily time. In what follows I will deal with a particular case of pathology: cyclical addiction, or more specifically cyclical alcoholism. Much has been written on this topic but little (certainly little that I can find) on its connections to brain rhythms[105], or; for that matter the genetic contributions to alcoholism.[106] Much has been written on alcohol's effects on the brain, but far less on the brain's effects on alcohol.

The example I will use is that of the novelist William Faulkner. My excuse is that I have long been fascinated with his writings and am familiar both with his life and with the influences on his writings. (That his stream of consciousness novels were significantly indebted to Bergson he admitted. He left us, however,

---

[104] Besides the well-known psychological effects of damage to the sleep cycle, there are also physiological effects, including an increased risk of cancer. Cf. D.G. Foster, "Are We Trying to Banish Biological Time?" *Cerebrum. Dana Foundation* (01 April 2004), 19, https://www.dana.org/article/are-we-trying-to-banish-biological-time/. Accessed 21 Feb 2022.

[105] An exception: R. Spanegal, A. Rosenwasser, Gunter Schumann, D. Sarkar, "Alcohol Consumption and the Body's Biological Clock," *Alcohol Clinical and Experimental Research* 29, no. 8 (2005): 1550-1557. Also Cf. "Biological Clock and Drug Addiction," *MEDICA Magazine* (2019). https://www.medica-tradefair.com/en/News/Archive/Biological_Clock_and_Drug_Addiction. Accessed 21 Feb 2022.

[106] The relations between genetics and alcohol consumption have been studied more than those of alcohol and brain rhythms. Cf. Donald W. Goodwin, "Alcoholism and Genetics, The Sins of the Fathers," *Archives of General Psychiatry* 42, no. 2 (1985): 171-174.

no account of the degree or nature of this influence[107].) The cyclic nature of Faulkner's alcoholism is described in detail by Joel Williamson, in his *William Faulkner and Southern History*.[108]Williamson gives us, almost a blow by blow account. Faulkner, Williamson contends, always took refuge from life in alcohol. It is the peculiar nature of that refuge that concerns us. That is, Faulkner's drinking fell into a pattern which Williamson describes as "cyclical": a recurrent rhythm which became predictable.[109] This became particularly acute beginning in his late 30's.[110] Henceforth the pattern was recurrent to the time of his death. He would experience long periods in which he did not drink. Then he would plunge into long periods of heavy drinking, ending in total collapse. "He mumbles," one of his friends reported after trying to help him, "can't control his bodily functions."[111] A stay at a hospital or asylum would put him back on his feet. Then for a long time he would not drink until suddenly alcohol consumption would begin again and continue until he fell into a state of total collapse. In the processes, he would be found wandering naked in hotel corridors, nearly drowning in a bath tub, or simply unconscious in bed.

Students of the behavior of alcoholics will find nothing new in this picture. It is common in many alcoholics, sometimes referred to as "binge drinking." In Faulkner's case it is particularly instructive, for at least three reasons: 1. It has a definite genetic component. (The Faulkner men had a history of heavy, sometimes uncontrollable drinking) 2. We are able to plot the periodicity of his drinking bouts with reasonable accuracy. 3. It is clear that his alcoholism was a mixture, a hybrid, of physical and psychological factors. Neither the physiological nor the psychological components of his illness can be studied independently. Williamson speculates that Faulkner's trouble was more psychological than physical.[112] If so, there is still the problem of why it took the recurrent cyclical form that it did. It is hard to believe that the timed, durational character of his drinking had nothing to do with genetics or with the temporal dynamics of the brain.

---

[107] Cf. Richard P. Adams, "The Apprenticeship of William Faulkner," *Tulane Studies in English*, Vol. 12 (Hassell Street Press, 1962): 113-155. For an extended bibliography on Bergson and Faulkner, see Pete A.Y. Gunter, *Henri Bergson: A Bibliography*. 2nd ed. (Bowling Green, OH: Philosophy Documentation Center, 1986), 533.

[108] Joel Williamson, *William Faulkner and Southern History* (New York: Oxford University Press, 1993), 509. (All future references to this work will be cited in the text as FSH.)

[109] FSH, 248, 257, 288, 349.

[110] FSH, 247.

[111] FSH, 286.

[112] FHS, 248.

Much more could be said about this example. Were there intrinsic connections between his cyclical alcoholism and the literary creativity of his sober periods? And what was the connection between his behavior and the genes he inherited from his ancestors? This is not merely a literary or biographical question. The study of the temporality of the body ought, one believes, lead to a better understanding of any number of pathologies, including alcoholism--perhaps, in the process, helping us to control it.

X.

Physics, Disorder, and Life

It may seem a long way from psychotherapy in its many forms to physics. That, however, is the direction which this study will take. Bergson's contributions to the arts and to psychology tend to be well known. His cosmological and physical thought have been submerged. One might say that they have been neglected. It would be more accurate to say that they have been regarded as implausible. What notions of matter or space or motion could be involved in a "vitalist" universe such as that portrayed in *Creative Evolution*? Doesn't his viewpoint transcend such mundane notions as measurement, physical determinism, the contributions of technological advance to experiment? Many of Bergsons's statements suggest this irrelevance. Thus:

> All the living hold together, and all yield to the same tremendous push. The animal takes its stand on the plant, man bestrides animality, and the whole of humanity, in space and time, is one immense army galloping beside and before and behind each of us in an overwhelming charge able to beat down every resistance and clear the most formidable obstacles, perhaps even death.[1]

An exhilarating passage, this literary ornament dramatically concludes chapter three of *Creative Evolution*, "The Meaning of Life." If it is an example of the kind of writing which helped make Bergson famous in his time, but which hardly reassured his scientifically-oriented readers.

As we have suggested in this essay, Bergson's rhetoric and his reliance on something as presumably vague as "duration" seem to many to lead to "metaphysics" in the worst sense of the word: that is, metaphysics as vague, sterile, and anti, or un-scientific. This impression (though it is easy to see how it could have arisen) is false. Bergson definitely had a physics. It is a necessary and inescapable result of his hierarchy of durations as I have repeatedly stressed. That is, as we descend from the durations of human experience through briefer and more spatially extensive durations we end, for Bergson with extraordinarily brief durations. These are the stuff of which matter, he holds, is made.

---

[1] CE, 173.

Our imagination is not at home with this view of matter, which we tend, almost inevitably, to view as made up of solid physical objects with definite shapes and unproblematic locations. This was the notion proposed by Isaac Newton and which dominated western science into the 1900s. Even now, though as a picture of the way the world works, it is hardly supported by quantum or relativity physics, physicists still fall back on it. But no matter how commonsense it is and no matter how deeply ingrained in our language, our sense organs and our behavior, it is a misleading image of nature. Much closer to our present physics is Bergson's view of matter as a series of pulses of energy. That is, but in a very broad way, his theory of matter presented first in *Matter and Memory* and developed in his later works bears a more than passing resemblance to today's quantum physics. I will discuss this resemblance later in this book. I would like to begin here, however, by once more discussing the relations between his thought and the science of thermodynamics. Here the French intuitionist was once again able to develop insights relative to today's sciences.

We have already mentioned thermodynamics in relation to both biology and to physical cosmology. It will help here to go into this science in greater detail. As noted above (Chapter 4), thermodynamics was created to account for the behavior of heat and was understood as describing a transition from order to disorder. Developed by Sadi Carnot to deal with heat engines, it was closely linked to the industrial revolution and the behavior of coal-burning machines. Victorian engineers were having a hard time understanding why were so inefficient. In the 1860s, Rudolf Clausius introduced the term "entropy" to quantify heat that was no longer available for doing useful work (e.g. driving a piston, as in the example of the struck match, energy is produced but the result is a heap of ashes.) Later in the century, Ludwig Boltzman gave thermodynamics its classical statement by formulating it in terms of statistics.

Thermodynamics has a single very clear implication: matter runs downhill. It tends, in using up energy (and producing entropy) towards increasing disorder. In the end, the Victorians believed, the universe would fall into a "heat death": a homogeneous nearly featureless flux and reflux of energy. It is not surprising that Bergson, at the turn of the twentieth century, should ask not where the descent of matter ends, but where it began: at a state of very high potential energy. This state, he insisted, resulted in a kind of thermodynamic dispersion: a vast expansion "into" space, creating and continuing to create stars, planets, galaxies, solar systems. And ultimately us.

A. New Beginning: The Thermodynamics of Ilya Prigogine

Bergon's speculations on thermodynamics and the origins of the universe, as I have said, went largely unnoticed in his time. They were, however, to be taken up again and made part of a new research program,[2] through the efforts of Ilya Prigogine, who was awarded a Nobel Prize for chemical kinetics in 1973.[3]

One of the surprising developments associated with the new thermodynamics is the discovery of previously unrecognized forms of organization termed "dissipative structures." On previous assumptions these should not exist. Near-equilibrium Boltzmanian thermodynamics predicts that from increasing energy exploitation there can be only two results: crystallization (a static order) or turbulence (an increasing disorder). It turns out, however, that in certain cases these results do not occur. Instead modes of dynamic order emerge. These include chemical waves (ring shaped waves, scroll waves, clockwise waves..) and chemical clocks.[4] These structures, it is suspected, could hold the answers to long unanswered questions in areas as diverse as biogenesis, embryogenesis, and brain function.[5] It turns out that most biochemical reactions are far from equilibrium.

On the negative side, this view contains an important limitative theorem. We are familiar with such theorems from both relativity and quantum physics. They place limits on the numbers that physicists can cite. In relativity no object can move faster than c, the speed of light. (To exceed this velocity would require infinite energy.) For quantum physics, it is impossible (via Heisenberg's uncertainty relations) to predict the exact position and momentum of an electron simultaneously. Prigogene's thermodynamics, similarly, forbids proceeding backward in time. Such processes involve measurement specifying infinite amounts of information. An "entropy barrier" renders infinite information impossible.[6] Travel into the past takes its place alongside perpetual motion machines as impossible.

On the positive side, the new thermodynamics pictures nature not as a collection of inert mass particles impelled by mechanical laws but as consisting of centers of chemical activity spontaneously giving rise to dynamic form. Far from equilibrium processes are thus in the fullest sense creative. They involve

---

[2] Pete A.Y. Gunter, "Bergson and Non-Linear Non-Equilibrium Thermodynamics: An Application Method," *Revue Internationale de Philosophie* 2, no. 177 (1991): 108-121.

[3] Ilya Prigogine and I. Stenger, *Order Out of Chaos* (New York: Bantam, 1984), 137-138. (All future references to this work will be cited in the text as OC.)

[4] Joseph E. Early, "Self-Organization and Agency: In Chemistry and in Process Philosophy," *Process Studies* 11, no. 4 (1981): 242-258.

[5] Y. Bouligand and J. Chanu, "Introduction biologique à la notion de structure dissipative," in *La Morphogénèse, de la biologie aux mathematiques*, ed. Y. Bouligand (Paris: Maloine, 1980), 39-44.

[6] OC, 295-297.

1. irreversibility in principle
2. macroscopic indeterminism
3. holism
4. multiplication of minor influence in mass phenomena.

By holism is meant not only that a minimum number of atoms or molecules are necessary for dissipative structures, but that the existence of such structures involves the influence of each of its components on all the others. In such a context the trajectory of an atom or molecule loses all simple location. One has only "ensembles" of trajectories.[7] Prigogine sums up this state of affairs as describing "the creative course of time."[8]

Probably the easiest way to visualize Prigogine's standpoint is by observing a surprising chemical phenomenon, the Belousov-Zaboutinksy reaction. This reaction was discovered by a Russian scientist Boris P. Belousov. His efforts to publish his discovery were met with rejection. (The second law of thermodynamics, he was told, forbade the emergence of dynamic form. Chemical processes should produce only disorder.) Belousov finally published in an obscure journal and let the matter rest.[9] Later another Russian physicist, Anatol Zabutinsky, discovered Belousov's paper, reformulated it, and made it acceptable to the scientific community. Henceforth Belousov's petri dish, filled with the correct chemicals, could be allowed to pulsate clocklike yellow and blue, or create intricate waves in what otherwise appears as an inert homogeneous mass.

The "BZ" reaction not only supports Prigogine's new thermodynamics, giving clear visible proof that nonlinear conditions can give rise to dynamic form. It suggests, for example, an explanation of the origin of life: By what magic does nature give rise to living cells? Science has so far failed to explain this process. Perhaps some as yet obscure factor describable only through nonlinear equations and their correlates, fractal form, will bring us closer to understanding what life is and how it emerges.[10]

It is interesting to look at how Prigogine came to create his new science. As a student with a broad background is history, archeology, music and philosophy he was struck by how differently time is treated in the humanities and the natural sciences. The two times, humanistic and physical, seemed to exist in two separate worlds. But surely they exist in the same world. Rejecting one

---

[7] OC, 261-264, 247-248, 273-274.

[8] OC, 307.

[9] As a Jewish scientist in Russia in the time of Stalin, he was probably wise to do so.

[10] Cf. Ilya Prigogine, *From Being to Becoming* (San Francisco: W.H. Freeman, 1980), 83-84. (All future references to this work will be cited in the text as FB)

while embracing the other seemed impossible. In the context of such perplexity the young scholar could find in Bergson's writings a brilliant analysis of the limitations of the, then, scientific approach to time and change and consider what follows if the alternative approach is accepted.

Another factor should be mentioned in relation to the development of Prigogine's thought: his reading of Albert Einstein. Prigogine's fascination with the great physicist dates, he tells us, from the same period as his study of Bergson. [11] In the Einstein-Bergson contrast the young scholar found two radically opposed approaches to the relations between being and becoming. In Einstein's case the contrast was even more radical. Einstein was flatly Eleatic. For him process, change, motion are only an illusion. At the April 1922 meeting of the Société française de Philosophie—as Prigogine notes[12]—Einstein rejected the Bergsonian problematic out of hand.[13] In this there is an element of justice, for Bergson had made errors in his interpretation of relativity. But, Prigogine argues, Bergson was right to protest against what Einstein's physics had left out.

> Can we say Bergson has failed in the same way the post-Kantian philosophy of nature failed? He has failed insofar as the metaphysics based on intuition has not materialized. He has not failed in that unlike Hegel, he had the good fortune to pass judgement upon a science that was, on the whole, firmly established--that is, a classical science at its apotheosis, and thus identified problems which are still our problems.[14]

When the author, many years ago now, questioned Prigogine about just what these persisting questions were and how the philosopher had failed to answer them he was very clear. For him, as opposed to Bergson, real creativity is found in nature or, rather, *in* matter. Prigogine states:

> In short Bergson's direction of thought was to oppose life and matter. My view is that life is deeply rooted in matter whenever the instability of dynamical systems and, closely related to this, autocatalytic reactions are taken into account.[15]

---

[11] Prigogine noted the importance of his early reading of both Bergson and Einstein at a conference on *Physics and the Ultimate Significance of Time* at Claremont, California, in March 1984. He admitted the same indebtedness in a letter to the author, 01 May 1989.

[12] OC, 204, 301-302.

[13] Cf. *Bulletin de la société française de philosophie* 22, no. 3 (1922): 102-113. Translated in *Bergson and the Evolution of Physics*, ed. and trans. Pete A.Y. Gunter (Knoxville: University of Tennessee Press, 1969), 123-135.

[14] FB, 3.

[15] Letter to the author, 1 May 1989.

Prigogine's critique is certainly understandable. The opposition between life and consciousness on the one hand and matter on the other is insisted on by Bergson throughout his oeuvre, most persistently in *Creative Evolution* where it becomes almost a mantra.[16] But did he really separate matter and consciousness? And did he make one the nemesis of the other?

The answer, as I have labored to show throughout this essay, is no. But Bergson certainly does not make it easy to see why this is not so. To make sense of the Bergsonian dilemma, it will help to take a glance at the Vitalist-Mechanist controversy, which first emerged in the Eighteenth century and held center stage throughout the Nineteenth century, only to subside and vanish early in the twentieth. Vitalists denied that life can be explained by matter or that physics holds the keys to biology. They held by contrast that a life force distinct from matter runs the affairs of the organism (or equally of evolution) from outside, as it were. Here we see the influence of Descartes, the ghost of his dualism casting its shadow across biology. Put in a nutshell, vitalists opposed a spiritual force to a mechanical materiality.

In spite of appearances and in spite of his reiterated opposition of memory and matter, life and geometrical extension, this is not Bergson's position. As we have seen Bergson opposes not spirit and mechanism but contrasting modes of duration. Matter, following the direction of the burnt match, tends towards the loss of form and an increasing incapacity to act. Life, following the direction of evolution, tends towards an increase of form, an increasing capacity for action. These, he insists, are only tendencies.[17] They are not predetermined either by some divine theological plan or by a Laplacian physical predeterminism. They are, to repeat the point, two kinds of duration. The difference between them is that not of two different sorts of substances.

How does this effect Prigogine's criticisms? Simply, Prigogine failed to understand Bergson's cosmology. If we look at Bergson's thought not from his repeated opposition of life and matter but in terms of his "big bang" cosmology, a very different picture emerges. As we have seen, Bergson speculates that matter was created and has "detended" in the direction of space[18] creating the astronomical order with which we are familiar. The universe, he argues, "is not made. It is being made continually. It is growing, perhaps indefinitely, by the addition of new worlds."[19] He states:

---

[16] E.g. CE, 64, 122-128, 236.

[17] CE, xiii, 4, 8.

[18] CE, 152.

[19] CE, 155.

> The life that evolves on the surface of our planet is indeed attached to matter. If it were pure consciousness, *a fortiori* if it were supraconsciousness, it would be pure creative activity. In fact, it is riveted to an organism that subjects it to the general laws of matter.[20]

Thus for Bergson if we were present an instant after the initial expansion of the universe, we would find not two universes--one vital and the other material--but a single universe embodying two contrasting tendencies: one exhibiting expenditures of energy and loss of structure, the other involving an increase in dynamic order. The latter would include both the development of solar systems and, subsequently, of living organisms. The contrast between life from matter would thus occur well after the universe's initial expansion. He is describing a bifurcation similar to that which will occur, repeatedly, in the course of biological evolution. In spite of the language he often uses, therefore, he is not opposing an independent vital force on one hand and an inert Newtonian matter on the other. Rather, he postulates two modes of duration which are interdependent.

If this is true, then "matter" is, far from Newton's world of inert mechanically interacting particles, remarkably rich, in itself and in terms of what it can produce.[21] Equally, if this is true then there would be reason to expect phenomena like the BZ reaction or the creativity that Prigogine and his colleagues find in innumerable chemical processes: that is, a transition from chaos to order. The so-called physics of chaos would then lend a partial verification to Bergson's ideas.

Few among the philosophers associated with the positivist Vienna circle wrote at any length about Bergson. An exception was Hans Reichenbach, who shared with Bergson a skepticism about the reversibility of time, and who therefore felt obliged to deal with the French philosopher's standpoint. In his *The Direction of Time*, Reichenbach gives a general description of Bergson's concept of temporality as it relates to thermodynamics and its laws. He concludes by simply dismissing Bergson's point of view, arguing that he fails to provide any basis for the investigation of entropy or any of the other concepts related to the use of energy. One cannot, Reichenbach argues, support one intuition by an appeal to another.

But we have seen that for Bergson to do philosophy is not simply to appeal from one intuition to another but to try to do so in contact with the data of the sciences at any one time. This might be, in the way that Bergson takes the

---

[20] CE, 158.

[21] The current "fractured" nature of physics will be examined along with a comparison of Bergson's physics with contemporary efforts to find unity.

intuition of duration into cosmology, broadening it so as to conceive the possibility of a "Big Bang" in cosmology. But on his terms our intuition can be deepened as well as broadened as when Ilya Prigogine was able to show that the production of entropy occurs consistently with the emergence of dynamic form. This deepens and transforms our sense of temporality as well as makes possible new scientific advances. The end of this book will present work from Jeremy England who expands provisional views to deal with the origin of life.

While Reichenbach's *The Direction of Time*[22] does tie Bergson's philosophy closely to thermodynamics, his comments, however, exhibit a serious misunderstanding of both Bergson's method and the results which he hoped would be reached by it. Even though Bergson's enthusiasm for a metaphysics of becoming may provide a good starting point for an investigation of thermodynamics, Reichenbach protests, it cannot replace such an investigation. For this, we must disregard philosophy and turn to physics, a science that Bergson, through his criticisms, has maligned. One cannot, Reichenbach argues, support one intuition by an appeal to another.

We are now in a position to understand why Bergson's philosophy leads to criticisms like Reichenbach's and at exactly what points Reichenbach's criticisms miss the mark. Bergson was not trying to discredit the natural sciences. He was trying to broaden them, render them more flexible, more applicable. His criticisms were certainly serious. In terms of Thomas Kuhn's paradigm shift hypothesis, by focusing on anomalies involved in the accepted paradigm, Bergson hoped to replace it with another. Such a scientific paradigm, he argues,

> ...could lead on deeper study to some other mode of analyzing the living being and so to a new discontinuity--although less removed, perhaps, from the real continuity of life.[23]

There is a vivid contrast between dead ends and new beginnings.

---

[22] Hans Reichenbach, *The Direction of Time*, ed. Maria Reichenbach (Chicago: University of Chicago Press, 1971), 16-17. There is almost nothing in the literature on the relations between Bergson and Reichenbach. An exception is Milič Čapek, *Bergson and Modern Physics* (Dordrecht-Holland: D. Reidel, 1971), 65-67, 272, 275-77, 350-53, 396.

[23] CE, 105.

XI.

Understandable Misunderstandings:
Early Anglo-American Receptions
of Bergson's Thought

Before dealing with Bergson's physics and his concepts of matter I would like to deal with something more general: that is, with the early reception of his thought by three prominent English-speaking philosophers: George Santayana, Bertrand Russell, and A.O. Lovejoy. There are two reasons for this focus. The first is that their criticisms (particularly Russell's) have left a misleading impression of Bergson, certainly in the English-speaking world. The second is that in correcting their misunderstandings one will not only arrive at a clearer picture of what Bergson actually said, but why what he said was so easy to misinterpret. This will help us better understand his physics and his biology. Even more, it will help us understand Bergson's historical context, which strongly influenced Russell's criticism.

The Anglo-American response to Bergson was in part not a response to Bergson but to his supposed allegiance to the spirit of his times: the *belle epoque*, the *fin de siècle*. The mentality of turn of the century Europe was a curious hybrid of optimism and anti-intellectualism. Though many at this time feared the onset of a disastrous war, more preferred to believe that in their time humanity had reached a pinnacle of development which pointed to a future of unparalleled discovery and creativity. Bergson's joint success as a lecturer and as a writer (particularly as the writer of *Creative Evolution*) made him appear to be both the symbol of that optimism and its spokesman. In this context it was easy to see him also as the archenemy of the stolid, backward-looking human intellect. In the words of Philippe Soulez and Frederic Worms, for better or for worse, Bergson was "in synch with the *Zeitgeist*."[1]

Part of Bergson's fame came, as I've noted, from an unlikely source: the notoriety of his lectures at the Collège de France. The notoriety of a series of lectures may seem a minor thing. But at that time Paris was the unquestioned center of world culture. A *cause célèbre* in Paris could quickly become a fad in

---

[1] Frederick Worms and Philippe Soulez, *Bergson* (Paris: Flammarion, 1997), 111. (All future references to this work will be cited in the text as B.)

London or New York: or for that matter, as it turned out, also in Paris. Popular success proved more vexing to him than flattering. Fashionable society women vied with frustrated students for seats at his lectures, who often could not find places from which to hear what their professor was saying. Many had to crawl into window spaces and hang half inside the lecture room, trying to steady themselves and take notes at the same time. To add to the increasing tumult the students protested to the university administration. In turn, the women protested to the students. All this boiled over into the press where both critics and enthusiasts vied in missing the point. One rag published an imaginary lecture on the Tango "...by the celebrated Metaphysician of the Collège de France, M. Bergson."[2] Journalists complained that Bergson's thought was merely "flattering to an idle and worldly public, to an audience composed for the most part of women."[3] It was suggested that his lectures be transferred to the Sorbonne auditorium or even the Paris Opera. In 1914 he ceased lecturing. His gesture and its meaning were largely ignored.

If on the one side Bergson's fame and influence involved the notion that his was a merely popular and "literary" exercise, on the other, it came to be viewed as an exercise in raw (and perhaps contradictory) political philosophy. My comments on this aspect of his reception and general impression will be brief.

To an English-speaking but not to a European audience the name George Sorel is not familiar. But among historians of twentieth century European politics and political theory it is remembered as the founder of syndicalism, with its call for the unity of the working class and its reliance on the general strike as a way of bringing the European power elite to its knees. Sorel had early attended Bergson's lectures and was an assiduous reader of *Creative Evolution.*[4] Bergsonian ideas are found throughout Sorel's works.[5] Sorel's political ideas were far more radical than Bergson's. Even so, Bergson's philosophy came to be incongruously identified in the public mind with both far left politics and aesthetic elitism. If that was not enough, while some of his followers used his ideas to defend their Catholicism, on June 1, 1914 his books were placed on the Roman Catholic Index and forbidden.

The results of this conflict were two. Many found it hard to find the real Bergson amidst the chorus of interpretations and counter-interpretations. The

---

[2] Gabrielle Reuillard, in *Les hommes du jour*, 371. Reuillard's article was quoted at length in *Current Opinion* LVI (May 1914). (All future references to this work will be cited as HJ.)

[3] HJ, 372.

[4] B, 114-121.

[5] Georges Sorel, *Reflections on Violence*, ed. J. Jennings (Cambridge: Cambridge University Press, 1999), 297. Also, *The Illusions of Progress* (Berkeley: University of California Press, 1969), 276.

result was, understandably, skepticism. Allied with this skepticism was the notion that Bergson was not an aesthetic elitist but something entirely intolerable and in terms of knowledge empty or worse: that is, a Mystic. The mystic attempts to say the unsayable. Hence, *Creative Evolution* must be simply a mystic poem, full of emotion, empty of meaning.

A. The Antibergsonian Polemic of George Santayana

George Santayana was one of three philosophers (The others were William James and Josiah Royce) who, as professors at Harvard University, presided over what many have called The Golden Age in American Philosophy. Not that Santayana was in agreement with his two eminent colleagues. He had no respect either for James's pragmatism or for any form of idealism, including Royce's. And he rarely lost an opportunity to say so.

This was particularly true of Bergson, whom he regarded as a typical product of a superficial age. His unmasking of the Bergsonian imposter appears in chapter three of *Winds of Doctrine: Studies in Contemporary Opinion* (1913).[6] Morris Grossman tells us that though Santayana's notes for this work are a tirade of "hasty hostility and capsule refutation," his published work is far more balanced and less acerbic than the original text.[7] If this is so, most of us would gladly forego reading the original. The more "balanced and muted" essay found in *Winds of Doctrine* is acidic enough.

Following the general tendency of this essay, I will concentrate not on Santayana's rhetoric but, more usefully, on the central points in which he simply and demonstrably failed to understand Bergson. These are three:

1. The belief that Bergson's thought is entirely subjectivist.
2. The closely related belief that on Bergson's terms nothing can be known about the world, which is featureless. And,
3. The belief that (because of Bergson's presumably neurotic fear of space) he proposed that the world is entirely unextended: there is neither space nor spatiality.

Santayana's primary assumption is that Bergson is a thoroughgoing subjectivist. By this he meant both that being wrapped in a veil of personal experiences,

---

[6] Georges Santayana, *Winds of Doctrine: Studies in Contemporary Opinion* (Kassel, Germany, EU: Parthenon Books, 2016), 157. Originally published in 1913. (All future references to this will be cited in the text as WD.)

[7] Morris Grossman, "A Glimpse at Some Unpublished Santayana Manuscripts," *Journal of Philosophy* 61, no.1 (1964): 61-69.

Bergson denies the existence of the external world; and that even if such a world did exist, we could know nothing about it. Santayana states:

> What now is M. Bergson's solution? That no articulable world, either material or psychical exists at all, but only a tendency or enduring effort to evolve images of both sorts...This solution is obtained by substituting, as usual, the ideas of the things for the things themselves and cheating the honest man who was talking about objects by answering him as if he were talking about himself.[8]

Bergson thus when he speaks of matter, explains it away, idealistically.[9] Without seeking to solve the only real problem of how nature is actively constituted, the French philosopher raises all the other problems artificially.

If one understands Bergson's concept of the levels of duration and of the human mind's ability to approximate to and participate in these levels, any notion of his presumed subjectivism vanishes. For him the experience of the world is a participation in that world. We participate in the rhythms and tonality of the rhythms of music as in those of a crowded room. This participation (of our duration in a multiplicity of others) which he anchors in "pure perception," is in things, not in us.[10] It is, to use Sartre's term, "*ec-static.*"

If our experience, as has been argued throughout this book, involves active participation and not a withdrawal into subjective fantasy, it would seem to follow that we can know something about that world. But on this point also, Santayana has no reservations:

> M. Bergson never reviews his facts in order to understand them, but only to discredit others who may have fancied they understood. He raises difficulties, he marks the problems that confront the naturalist and the inadequacy of explanations that may have been suggested. Such criticism would be a valuable beginning if it were followed by the suggestion of some new solution; but the suggestion is only that no solution is possible, that the phenomena of life are simply miraculous...[11]

---

[8] WD, 72-72. Santayana was not alone in his view, which was shared by many scientists, e.g. Marcel Herubel, "Review of *L'évolution créatrice* by Henri Bergson," *L'année biologique* 15 (1910): 532-35. Harubel concludes that Bergson's work leaves scientists no farther along than they were originally.

[9] WD, 75.

[10] MM, 84, 297.

[11] WD, 51-52.

With such a philosophy of science, he concludes, all progress in scientific understanding would come to an end as it did after Aristotle.[12]

A useful response to Santayana at this point would be to show, as we have endeavored to do earlier in this essay, that Bergson's insights into duration and various of its aspects have been able to engender new (and valid) scientific concepts. Another response would be to cite Bergson's actual texts--texts which Santayana systematically neglects--in which the conceptual fruitfulness of intuition is categorically affirmed. For example, in *An Introduction to Metaphysics* he states:

> A careful study of the history of human thought would show that to it (ie. intuition) we owe the greatest accomplishments in the sciences, as well as what living quality there is in metaphysics. The most powerful method of investigation known to the human mind, the infinitesimal calculus, was born of that very reversal.[13]

On the next page, he argues that intuition, in its reversal of our usual modes of thought, finds modes of expression in abstract concepts. Thus, revolutionary periods of science begin with fundamental insights which can be formulated in (perhaps new) symbolism. These, if shown to be valid, will describe the real world more accurately.[14]

Santayana's refusal to deal in detail with Bergson's actual statements is one of the strangest aspects of his argument. At the very least he should have cited passages in, say, *Creative Evolution* or *An Introduction to Metaphysics* which affirm the positive relations between intuition and knowledge. That he fails entirely to do so is a real weakness.

This said, it is easy to see why Santayana was led to take the position that he did. If one reads *Creative Evolution* simply in terms of its life force or *élan vital* it is easy to construe Bergson's thought as little more than a literary exercise: "verbiage," "verbial mythology," or a mere "hypostasis of words."[15] Consider the following passage, in which Bergson compares biological evolution to the creativity of a poet putting his inspiration into verse:

> But through the words, lines and verses runs the simple inspiration which is the whole poem. So [in evolution] among the associated individuals, one life goes on moving: everywhere the tendency to individualize is opposed and at the same time completed by an

---

12 WD, 52.

13 CM, 225.

14 CM, 226.

15 WD, 71.

antagonistic and complementary tendency to associate, as if the manifold unity of life, drawn in the direction of multiplicity, made so much more the effort to withdraw itself into itself.[16]

In one respect, this is a useful metaphor intended to shed light on the way in which similar developmental tendencies occur on different branches of the evolutionary tree. But it is clearly literary. On the basis of it and similar metaphors scattered in *Creative Evolution*, Santayana concludes not only that Bergson's is a literary psychology[17] but that his biology is a literary biology. It would then be a cosmic poem uttered by a mystical One: no doubt full of sound and fury but signifying nothing.

Here again Santayana needed to deal in depth with what Bergson actually wrote. In relation to Bergson's merely literary prose, he might have read the passages in *An Introduction to Metaphysics* in which the uses of imagery are dealt with systematically and skeptically. Images may aid us, he states, in "getting into" duration. But they can mislead us. After providing several examples of images which might provide fundamental insight,[18] he cautions against taking any one image literally:

> In this regard, the philosopher's sole aim should be to start up a certain effort which the utilitarian habits of mind of everyday life tend, in most men, to discourage. Now the image has at least the advantage of keeping us in the concrete. No image will replace the intuition of duration, but many different images, taken from quite different orders of things, will be able, through the convergence of their action, to direct consciousness to the precise point where there is a certain intuition to seize on.[19]

What is needed is an interplay of contrasting images that by their very differences can help us to focus on fundamental change.[20]

One may disagree with Bergson's description of the part which images play in reaching philosophical insight. But it is clear that he has thought about the problem of images and explained how he intends to use imagery.[21] *An Introduction to Metaphysics* is the introduction to the metaphysics of *Creative Evolution*. The

---

[16] CE, 166.

[17] WD, 57, 64-65, 72f.

[18] These are: the rolling up and unrolling of a spool or thread, the spectrum, a piece of stretched elastic (CM, 192-194).

[19] CM, 195.

[20] CM, 192-94.

[21] Cf. Lydie Adolphe, *La dialectique des images chez Bergson* (Paris: Presses Universitaires de France, 1951), 380.

role that imagery plays in *Creative Evolution* was thought out ahead of time and applied systematically there.

We should not be surprised, then, to read Bergson's warning in *Creative Evolution*. The vital impetus, he states, is only an image. But, he adds, "...it must be compared to an image, because no image borrowed from the physical world can give more nearly the idea of it. But it is only an image.[22] Like all images, it will need to be complemented by others which contrast with it in order to give a fuller notion of biological evolution. It would need to be understood; for example, in terms of its branching or bifurcating character, which we have encountered through the imagery of fractal geometry. A fuller grasp of the dynamic of evolution would add the "fall"[23] of life into space, a descent we might view through the imagery of fractal dimensions. Bergson's images in *Creative Evolution* (rockets, falling ashes...) are an attempt to provide insight, not to provoke mystification.[24]

Finally, we come to Santayana's account of Bergson's concepts of space and of extension generally. It is clear to Santayana that this account is not based on reasoning but has roots in Bergson's severe psychological problems. That is, Bergson suffers from "cosmic agoraphobia."[25]

> M. Bergson is afraid of space, of mathematics, of necessity; and of eternity; he is afraid of the intellect and of the possible discoveries of science: he is afraid of nothingness and death.[26]

What Bergson dreads in space is that the heart should be obsessed by it and transformed into it.[27]

But if Bergson suffers from spatial phobia he certainly does not apply it to his philosophy, which makes abundant room for space and extensity. His temporal hierarchy does not exist outside of space. The opposite is true. Each step down his temporal scale involves increasing extension, tending towards and closely approximating ordinary Euclidean space. The result is unmistakable. For the French philosopher, everything that exists has spatial extensity.

Nothing real is unextended.

---

[22] CE, 165.

[23] "Fall," it should be pointed out, suggests ordinary imagery.

[24] In the next section, following the account of Bergson's early reception by English-speaking philosophers, it will be argued that Bergson's reflections on the vitality of evolution can be developed in the direction of science.

[25] WD, 48.

[26] WD, 49.

[27] WD, 48.

On this point too Santayana could have saved himself a lot of ink and many lines of diatribe. Spatiality for Bergson is not "only imagined"[28] as Santayana has it. It is not a dead category like "space, matter, mind, truth or person."[29] It is quite real, as is matter. There is not the slightest indication that Bergson lived in metaphysical fear of either matter or space. If this were so, why did he go to such lengths to affirm the existence of both?

B. Bertrand Russell on Bergson: Bats, Bees, and Knowledge

It is hard to imagine a thinker less like George Santayana than Bertrand Russell. Where Santayana is essentially a literary aesthetician, Russell is a logician. Where Santayana sought to live only "the austere life of the mind," Russell passionately involved himself in political movements: passivism and socialism, for two. But if the two philosophers diverged in their concept of philosophy, they united in their distaste for Bergson. Bergson, Russell insisted, is opposed to any kind of reasoning whatsoever. When his philosophy has triumphed "...it is to be supposed that argument will cease, and intellect will be lulled to sleep on the heaving sea of intuition."[30]

The beliefs which led Russell to this conclusion are many. I will deal with only two here: 1. his treatment of intuition as a form of instinct, with all the limitations of instinct 2. his assumption that there is no real distinction between any entities in Bergson's universe, only a seamless and unbroken continuity: which swallows everything 3. his denial that Bergson finds a way of explaining how we can apply mathematics successfully to nature. The first two of these issues will be dealt with here. The third will be explored in the section dealing with Bergson's understanding of physics.

1. Instinct and Russell

Intuition, Russell writes, is at its best "in bats, bees, and Bergson."[31] Probably in dogs, Russell states, it exceeds anything to be found in humans.[32] This interpretation of Bergson's concept of instinct is accompanied by a quote from Bergson which clearly contradicts Russell's opinions but which Russell then

---

[28] WD, 64.

[29] WD, 68.

[30] Bertrand Russell, *The Philosophy of Bergson, With a Reply by H. Wildon Carr and a Rejoinder by Bertrand Russell* (Cambridge: Bowes and Bowes, 1914), 36. (All future references to this work will be cited in the text as PB.)

[31] Bertrand Russell, *Mysticism and Logic and Other Essays* (London: Allen & Unwin, 1910), 3. (All future references to this work will be cited in the text as ML.)

[32] ML, 11.

ignores. That is, Bergson states that intuition is instinct which has been "...made disinterested, self-conscious, and capable of reflecting on its object and enlarging it indefinitely."[33] As we will see, actual instinct as found in animals (particularly insects) is anything but disinterested or reflective or broad.

To see this will require a glance at the place of instinct in the complex of divergences which for Bergson constitute evolution. Having introduced the term "intuition" in *An Introduction to Metaphysics*, he feels obliged in *Creative Evolution* to see it in its biological context. In doing so, he makes every effort to describe instinct in its biological context, which is quite different from that of intuition per se.

The first major split in the evolutionary process, Bergson states, was the separation of the animal and plant Kingdoms.[34] The second was the split between vertebrates and invertebrates. Bergson pays particular attention to the arthropods,[35] which are distinguished from the vertebrates by their external or exoskeleton. Bergson thinks this divergence has important implications for what, and how, organisms can know.

The evolution of the vertebrates, Bergson holds, involves the gradual development of a brain and nervous system which enables them to manipulate solid objects. Man is the ultimate outcome of this process. Human beings are, par excellence, the manipulators of solids. By contrast, arthropods, whose culmination is found, he believes, in the social insects, are focussed in their behavior on a knowledge of living things. This knowledge can be remarkably precise:

> The Scolia, which attacks a larvae of the rose beetle, stings it at one point only, but in this point the motor ganglia are concentrated and these ganglia alone: the stinging of other ganglia might cause death and putrification which it must avoid. The yellow winged Sphex, which has chosen the cricket as its victim, knows that the cricket has three nerve centers which serve its three pairs of legs--or at least it acts as if it knew this. It stings the insect first under the neck, then behind the prothorax, and then where the thorax joins the abdomen.[36]

The goal of these surgically accurate behaviors is to secure meat for the Scolia's and the Sphex's larvae. However grim we may find such scenarios, they exhibit,

---

[33] CE, 186.

[34] CE, 84.

[35] CE, 92-93.

[36] CE, 111.

Bergson believes, a kind of knowledge. It is not unerring. Insects can make mistakes: killing instead of paralyzing their victims, for example. (CE11) Instinct suffers also from narrowing focus, dealing as it does with only very specific aspects of its prey. The Sphex is not interested in the cricket's *élan vital* but only in its parts, the manipulation of which produces paralysis. In doing so it acts as a behavioral triphammer. Its function is to start in motion a process that is repetitive, almost mechanical. Bergson observes, "Riveted to the object of its practical interest, it is turned but by it into movements of locomotion."[37] In its function, there is nothing at all in instinct that is profound, or reflective.

If this is true, then Bergson's intuition cannot possibly be instinct. Intuition has breadth of vision. It can, if he is right, deal with the nature of life, the character of evolutionary divergence, the entropic fall of matter. Instinct by contrast has tunnel vision. In each case it deals with one or a highly restricted number of factors, and nothing else. Equally telling, where intuition seeks no immediate use (It sees for the sake of seeing.), instinct has an immediate pragmatic function: it involves "the utilization of a specific instrument for a specific object."[38] Finally, where instinct endlessly repeats the past, intuition as Bergson amply explains, makes new openings to the future.

2. Continuity Unmasked

No interpreter of Bergson would deny that the notion of continuity is fundamental to his philosophy. From the beginning of his career to the end, the continuity of duration is championed over and against the discontinuity of points in space and instants of clock time. It would appear to follow from this that Bergson's world-in-duration has no place for particulars and no way of distinguishing present from either past or future. It is not hard to find passages in his writings which are hard to interpret in any other way. Thus, in *Creative Evolution* he proclaims:

> Yet a beneficent fluid bathes us, whence we draw the very force to labor and to live. From the ocean of life, in which we are immersed we are continually drawing something, and we feel that our being, or at least the intellect that guides it, has been formed therein by a kind of local concentration. Philosophy can only be an effort to dissolve into the Whole.[39]

---

[37] CE, 115.

[38] CE, 91.

[39] CE, 123.

One can imagine Russell responding that it would be good if people like Bergson did get absorbed into the Whole: and thus disappear. Or, another example: "...things once constituted, show that on their surface, by their changes in situation the profound changes that are being accomplished in the whole."[40] But if this is true, there would appear to be no distinct things (rocks, rivers, trees...) in the world. Another way of putting this would be to say that if only the whole can act, the parts are at best passive components of the whole.

If this is true of the things existing at the same time (that is, in space or spatially related) it is equally true, Russell asserts, for things appearing in succession (that is, in time or duration):

> Life, in this philosophy is a continuous stream, in which all divisions are artificial and unreal. Separate things, beginnings and endings, are mere convenient fictions: there are only smooth unbroken transitions.[41]

This imperviousness to distinctions is for Russell what renders Bergson conceptually destructive. Though reality can be *lived*, for Bergson, according to Russell, it cannot be *thought*.[42] That is why logic, mathematics and physics "disappear" in this philosophy.

Russell takes the example of the moving arrow as a case in point. Does the arrow really move? Zeno argues that there is an arrow, but since it is always stationary at a point, it does not move. For Bergson and Heraclitus, Russell states there is motion, but arrows do not exist: that is, there are no things that change.[43] But a brief sketch of Bergson's physics shows that he never accepted the view that physical objects are illusions. An arrow (or a bullet or a rock) is for him is ultimately comprised of very brief rhythms of duration. A fuller account of his picture of matter will be given at the end of this essay. Enough has been said to indicate that real arrows with their material components (electrons, atoms, molecules) exist for Bergson.

If Bergson's conception of duration's continuity does not preclude the existence of arrows, neither does it exclude the existence of aspects of discontinuity in the flow of things. We have already discussed these as rhythms of duration. The rhythmic character of duration helps us to distinguish one rhythm form the next, and in objectively marking out beginnings, middles, and endings. To do so does not depend on there being mathematical points or instants in nature. We are able to make the before-after distinction and many others

---

[40] CE, 193.

[41] ML, 15.

[42] ML, 15.

[43] DB, 10, 13, 18.

without them. As I hope to show, both in a coming discussion of both biological evolution and of physical theory in Bergson, the distinguishability of successive epochs is for him not an illusion introduced by the meddling intellect but a fundamental fact of nature. That it lends itself to mathematical descriptions is what Bergson expects.

More needs to be said about Russell's interpretation. But enough has been said here to indicate where it falls short. Bergson is not the philosopher of a featureless amorphous becoming. Becoming whether a matter of present or successive moments, has natural articulations which allow us to make grounded distinctions. Equally, Bergson does not say that reality can only be lived, not thought. He believes it is possible to *think* in and about duration. To do so is to bring both intelligibility and effective consequences into existence.

3. A.O. Lovejoy: The Contradictions of Duration

Arthur Oncken Lovejoy (1873-1962), professor at Johns Hopkins University and for many years a prominent figure in the American scholarly scene, was both a philosopher and a historian of ideas. His interest in Bergson's philosophy persisted over a quarter of a century, from *Bergson and Romantic Evolutionism* (1914) through *The Reason, The Understanding and Time* (1939).[44] In contrast with Russell and Santayana, Lovejoy found some aspects of Bergson's thought congenial. Even so, others of the French philosopher's ideas he found unacceptable. Moreover, unlike Russell and Santayana, he contacted Bergson personally to give his French colleague a chance to answer his objections directly. Granted the differences between Lovejoy's general view of Bergson and those of Russell and Santayana, on some fundamental issues the three scholars agree. All complain of Bergson's anti-intellectualism.[45] All lament his appeal to the "ineffable."[46] Most important of all, Lovejoy joins his colleagues in denying that for Bergson there is a real, material world (or—if there is—that philosophy cannot deal with it): "But, as we have seen, the material world is not the true reality revealed in intuition, and the life of action is not the road to metaphysical knowledge."[47] Lovejoy cites Bergson's appeal to pure perception (which constitutes for Bergson the mind's contact with the rhythms of matter); however, he only notes

---

[44] A.O. Lovejoy, *Bergson and Romantic Evolutionism*, (Berkeley: University of California Press, 1914), 61. (All future references to this work will be cited in the text as BRE.); *The Reason the Understanding and Time* (Baltimore: The Johns Hopkins Press, 1961), 210. This item consists of lectures delivered in 1939. (All references to this work will be cited in the text as RUT.)

[45] RUT, 27f.

[46] RUT, 39-40.

[47] RUT, 91.

that Bergson turns from it to stress the reality of pure memory that preserves the entirety of our past. That Bergson proposes that we can have a direct encounter with (i.e. an intuition of) the world around us *via* pure perception is denied or simply misunderstood.

Besides the criticisms he shared with Russell and Santayana (which by the time Lovejoy wrote had become a chorus among academics), Lovejoy offered, to his credit, specific criticisms, which his allies did not explicitly address. That is, he attempted to show that the very idea of duration is self-contradictory. He sums up these contradictions in a brief passage:

> ...a duration to which the concept of quantity is inapplicable, a temporal succession in which there can be no mutual externality of the successive moments, a 'memory' in which the event remembered and the experience of remembering it are simultaneous--these appear to be perfect examples of the assertion of logically irreconcilable predicates of identical subjects.[48]

Lovejoy's critical passage harbors a number of objections. I will deal first with his claim that there cannot be succession unless its moments are external to each other. I myself, he insists, "...can only say that I have never experienced a melody in which the notes had no 'distinct and numerical multiplicity'..."[49] Here, Lovejoy is categorical. Notes cannot be merely different or distinguishable in order to afford a melody. They *absolutely* must be distinct.

Lovejoy's denial stems, I believe, from his failure to deal with the contrast between "distinct" and "distinguishable." It is quite possible for two objects of perception to be distinguished without their being perfectly distinct. Nothing, in fact is more common, even if the objects are spatial, not temporal. Take the visual spectrum. We easily distinguish blue from green in the spectrum even though we can find no sharp boundary between them. To use another example, impressionist paintings contain innumerable instances of shadings in which we are able to make distinctions without encountering distinct boundaries. We often perceive the tree bough as one while clearly being able to distinguish the multiplicity of its leaves.

But when we turn from spatial to auditory (hence temporal) examples we find the same thing: an experience of continuity coupled with an ability to make distinctions. Take for example the clarinet glissando which introduces Gershwin's "Rhapsody in Blue." Here there is succession. If there were not there would be no glissando. But given its dynamic continuity we can still make distinctions between its regions: earlier, middle, or later for example. Moreover, we make these distinctions in duration as the music unfolds. This provides a clear

---

[48] RUT, 147.
[49] RUT, 192.

counterexample to Lovejoy's claim that numerical multiplicity is necessary to our hearing a melody.

A glissando, if it exhibits specific regions, does not contain notes. It is also, Lovejoy might complain, not a melody. So let us take a melody in which notes predominate, the first four notes of Beethoven's fifth symphony (often summed up as "Fate knocks at the door"). No one would object that in this example there are no distinguishable notes. Beethoven's notes stand out so strongly from their background that they are impossible to neglect. But unless they occur in succession, they cannot constitute a melody.[50] There must, for the melody to emerge, be internal relations[51] between its components; such that the second note is changed in its character by its relation to the first, the third by its relation to the second. The developing continuity of a melody cannot exist without its components. But if its components are distinct like a number in a series or a note in a musical score, the melody vanishes. Bring back dynamism and continuity, and the melody returns. Also, *contra* Lovejoy, we have no difficulty in distinguishing notes from each other in Beethoven's qualitative, dynamic (if dramatic) continuity.

If Bergson's response to Lovejoy failed to convert the American thinker, it is not hard to see why. When we pronounce a phrase all at once, Bergson states, without introducing punctuation:

> ...we have, once more, the clear feeling of a succession without before or after, the feeling of a solid—by which I mean indivisible—duration. Now, in precisely the degree in which we make a greater effort of attention to resume possession of ourselves, to that degree we tend to perceive our inner life which 'expands' without ever permitting divisions, in absolutely the same way as a continuing melody.[52]

But Bergson here overstates his own position. He cannot mean that the beginning of a conversational phrase and its ending occur at the same instant. In a conversation the start of a phrase precedes its ending. Once it is completed, however, we are entitled to state that a phrase once completed is a given *at once*, without a before or after and in this sense refer to it as "solid." We are also entitled on Bergson's viewpoint to claim that a phrase has no divisions, if we mean absolutely distinct divisions or sections. But we are not entitled to say

---

[50] They would constitute a third, as other melodies might display a chord (if taken simultaneously).

[51] An internal relation is one in which the terms are changed by being in that relationship. An external relation is one which in no way affects its terms.

[52] RUT, 186.

that it has no *distinguishable* components: in the case of a phrase, no distinguishable words.[53]

Those familiar with Bergson will recognize the distinctions I have just urged against his response to Lovejoy as distinctions which he himself often makes: particularly between an act while it is being performed and an act after it has been performed and is thus complete. Bergson is right to insist, against his American critic, that questions concerning the nature of time cannot be answered without attending closely to the experience of duration. That experience, however, besides being experienced must be interpreted. The problem is that in writing Lovejoy not only does Bergson leave out distinctions which he himself had developed, he fails to discuss characteristics of duration (rhythms of duration, hierarchies of duration) which he has also developed, and which would have helped to explain his thought.

In the next section, which deals with Bergson's philosophy and physics, I will once again deal with questions raised by Lovejoy's response. This will involve a return to and amplification of the concept of durational hierarchy, which, it turns out, is remarkably rich, involving both the concept of "passage to the limit" analogous to that found in the calculus and a description of the degrees of connectivity between different rhythms of duration. These in turn will cast a revealing light on his philosophy, answering questions which otherwise seem to lack an answer.

To see the applicability and the plausibility of his ideas it will be necessary to deal, however schematically, with ideas in basic physics. To these I will now turn.

---

[53] We could not, if this were the case, distinguish one phrase from another.

XII.

Second Interlude:
Why We Can Measure Nature

The main goal of this book has been to show how, starting from an intuition of duration we can come to understand things that we would otherwise be unlikely to see, and, having seen them, to understand them with precision. The prior chapter was an exception to that rule. It was a critique of Bergson's anglophone critics, who assumed that the process in his thought that leads from intuition to novel modes of analysis is impossible, incomprehensible, even laughable. On this point they missed the point. I have tried to show in what ways they did so, and why.

The present chapter, which is an interlude in itself as well as a prelude to the next two chapters, on physics and biology respectively, is significantly different from its predecessor. Here the centerpiece is mathematics or more precisely, the question of how the world can be successfully described mathematically. On Bergson's terms this must seem unlikely. The universe, he insists, is comprised of durations and durations are qualitative. How then can it be depicted with numbers if numbers, as he states, both static and discrete? How can the moving arrow be said to move if time, space and motion are made up for immobile points, lines, and instants? If this is so, mathematical descriptions of the world must be illusory. This does seem to be Bergson's position. Mathematics, he seems to be saying, distorts the given. Starting with experienced mobility it ends with a world devoid of motion.

But there is another problem, closely connected to the first. How is it that a world so rich in qualitative character (think of the smell of a rose) can be described effectively with our measurements and our equations? I once heard the physicist Eugene Wigner put it in a simple but memorable phrase: how can we explain "the unreasonable effectiveness of mathematics"? How is it that the complex very abstract relations studied by mathematicians can so concretely and accurately describe the order of nature and give us such power over it? Wigner did not provide an answer.

Bergson produced, however, a way of resolving both of these problems. He was able to show through the concept of duration itself, how a world comprised of durations will display characteristics which both invite and justify quantitative measurement. To deal with this will involve a return to the notion of durational hierarchy but from a new point of view. We have seen that this concept can help us deal with scientific ideas (e.g. biological time) as well as phenomenologically oriented investigations (e.g. the theory of perception). Here we will find that it can be applied in another way: that is, in helping us understand the basis of our knowledge. It therefore has an *epistemological* use.

We recall the fundamental concepts of the hierarchy of duration: rhythms of duration and the elation of extending over. With these notions we can generate a durational hierarchy, creating a series of durations each briefer than its successor. We have seen, for example, how this notion can help us to deal with the rhythms of matter. At the limits of the hierarchy where we deal with the briefest durations, we get a concept of the physical world as made of brief, almost repetitive, processes. This series approximates instants of time, but never attains them. For the moment here we can disregard discussions of physics and simply deal with this limit concept and its approximation to an instant as a way of understanding how we can apply mathematics to nature—to the world. The hierarchy of durations thus becomes an instrument of knowledge generally.

It is important to see that even though the limit of the series is never reached, its existence is by no means merely arbitrary. As in the following (if spatial) example, the terminus of the series is framed by the elements that precede it. The limit case, the "limit" of the series, though ideal, is picked out or pointed to by the members in the series which preceded it. It is as inescapable as it is ideal.

At least two things follow from treating points and instants as limit cases. The first is that the applicability of our mathematics to the world suddenly becomes intelligible. The physical world does not have to consist of geometrical extension, as, for example, Descartes thought, in order for mathematical physics to succeed. There are innumerable facts which in their multiplicity, constitute converging series. (I will give examples of these immediately below.) Nature "frames" lives, points, and instants quite naturally. The second is that once this approach is taken, it turns out to be surprisingly near to common sense, common experience.

For example, in an ordinary room the place where the wall and the ceiling meet constitutes a straight line. A close look, of course, will reveal that it is not perfectly so. Irregularities (of paint, wallpaper, carpentry) show up all too often. Yet the wall-ceiling meeting point is still justifiably termed straight. As adjacent areas of wall and ceiling become progressively smaller, converging on their intersection, straightness becomes increasingly clear. It exists as an idealization but an idealization "framed" by the physical world itself. A simple example can be found in the pistol shot that starts a race. Is it instantaneous? Strictly speaking, no. But there is a natural convergence of briefer sounds (crowd noise, conversation, the sounds of the runners crouching in their blocks) which frame the "instant" of the gunshot. We can thus say that the race began at the gunshot as time "t." The many surrounding rhythms in the stadium depict it.

It is a long way from these ordinary examples to quantum measurement or the prediction of an eclipse. But the principle is the same. Converging sets of natural phenomena point towards limits which are of a particular place and time and not elsewhere. Measurement and the use of points and instants is well grounded. But we should not conclude, on this account, that instants and points are real entities in the world.

Bergson developed the notion of temporal hierarchy in 1896 in *Matter and Memory*. It is fascinating to see the same idea developed later by the English philosopher and mathematician Alfred North Whitehead. Where Bergson describes this temporal hierarchy in very general terms and does not go into specifics, Whitehead is at pains to present a detailed logical analysis. What follows is an extended excerpt from his *An Enquiry Concerning the Principles of Natural Knowledge*.

27. The Relation of Extension, Fundamental Properties.

27.1 The fact that event a extends over event b will be expressed by the abbreviation aKb. Thus 'K' is to be read 'extends over' and is the symbol for the fundamental relation of extension.

27.2 Some properties of K essential for the method of extensive abstraction are,

   (i)   aKb implies that a is distinct form b, namely, 'part' here means 'proper part':

   (ii)   Every event extends over other events and is itself part of other events: the set of events which an event e extends over is called the set of parts of e:

   (iii) If the parts of b are also parts of a and a and b are distinct, then aKb:

   (iv)   The relations K is transitive, i.e. if aKb and bKc, then aKc

   (v)   If aKc, there are events such as b where aKb and bKc:

   (vi)   If a and b are any two events, there are events such as e where eKa, and eKb.[1]

---

[1] Alfred North Whitehead, *An Enquiry Concerning the Principle of Natural Knowledge*, 2nd ed. (Eastford, CT: Martino Fine Books, 2017), 101. (All future references to this work will be cited in the text as PKN.) This second edition was originally published in 1924.

Whitehead's concept of abstractive classes, though more fully developed, is all but identical with Bergson's notion of temporal hierarchy. Most significantly, his series is composed of durations (events, in his terms), not of units of space. That Whitehead provides a careful logical analysis of the concept is helpful. But Bergson would, I believe, have accepted Whitehead's analysis as making explicit what is presumed in his notion of temporal hierarchy: for example, the transitive nature of relations between hierarchical levels, and the manner in which events (durations) can participate in more than one series. A year after *An Enquiry into the Principles of Natural Knowledge*, 1920, Whitehead published a second book, *The Concept of Nature*,[2] which contains a chapter on extensive abstraction. Bergson, who read *The Concept of Nature*, makes clear his delight with Whitehead's approach, terming it the most profound work "ever written on the philosophy of nature."[3]

Whitehead makes it clear that an abstractive set, like Bergson's hierarchy of durations, converges towards a limit which does not exist, yet is justified in its application to that context: "...an abstractive set as we pass along it converges to an ideal of all nature with no temporal extension...But this ideal is the ideal of a nonentity."[4] But the elements of the converging series depends on the progressive simplicity of the actual components of nature. The order of these diminishing durations is made possible through the progressive simplicity of the rhythms of nature. We are thus justified in stating that the race starts at 't' by the converging sets of duration in the stadium.

Whitehead's vision of nature, like Bergson's, is that of an array of rhythms, from the longer to the briefer:

> Molecules are non-uniform objects and as such exhibit a rhythm: although, as known to us, it is a rhythm of excessive simplicity. Living bodies exhibit rhythm of the greatest subtlety within our apprehension.[5]

The manner in which organisms (or for that matter molecules) are comprised of levels of duration is also made clear: "Thus every great rhythm presupposes lesser rhythms without which it could not be. No rhythm can be founded upon mere confusion or mere sameness."[6] Whitehead also embraces the notion of biological time, so central to Bergson's thought. He even distinguishes, as

---

[2] Alfred North Whitehead, *The Concept of Nature* (Cambridge: At the University Press), 1955, Ch. IV, 74-98. (All future references to this work will be cited in the text as CN.)

[3] DS, 62n.

[4] CN, 61.

[5] PNK, 199.

[6] PKN, 198.

Bergson does, between the temporality of matter and that of living things. Though both are processes: "Life is the rhythm as such, whereas a physical object is an average of rhythms which build no rhythm in their aggregation; and thus matter is in itself lifeless."[7] It is no wonder that Bergson should have taken such pleasure in finding that so acute and knowledgeable a contemporary thinker as Whitehead had developed a concept of nature and of scientific thought so close to his own.

But the matter goes well beyond the recognition of similarity. In a letter to Milič Čapek in 1938, Bergson notes that Whitehead was the only philosopher who understood his physics.[8] One can imagine his frustration over the failure by philosophers and scientists to understand his thought. In his letter, he adds that though his ideas were disregarded, he believed when he formulated them that they were "...in the direction in which sooner or later physics would move."[9]

I cannot resist ending this study on a note of irony. In the previous chapter, a brief account of Bertrand Russell's attack on Bergson was presented. Clearly, Russell had no use for Bergson or any part of his philosophy. It is all the more striking given the harshness of Russell's critique, that in *Our Knowledge of the External World*, a set of Russell's lectures delivered in 1914, he embraces Whitehead's theory of extensive abstraction, using it to explain how mathematical concepts like points and instants can be derived from concrete experience. Russell accepts the method of extensive abstraction as a way of making philosophy scientific at last.[10] One wonders what he would have said if he had known that Bergson had hit on the same idea, and used it to understand scientific research (e.g. into biological and physical time) and that Whitehead had profited, in formulating his own theory by considering the ideas of Bergson.

---

[7] PNK, 197.

[8] Henri Bergson, "Lettre à Milič Čapek July 3, 1938," *Correspondences*, ed. André Robinet (Paris: Presses Universitaires de France, 2002), 1596-7. Also, for an excellent analysis of the similarities between Bergson and Whitehead, see Milič Čapek, *Bergson and Modern Physics* (Dordrecht: D. Reidel, 1971), 267-268, 303-309. (All future references to this work will be cited in the text as BMP).

[9] BMP, xi: "...*en même temps dans la direction* où la physique engagerait tôt or tarde."

[10] Bertrand Russell, *Our Knowledge of the External World*, (Coppell, Tx: Didactic Press, 2017), 88-94.

XIII.

Bergson's Physics:
Speculations Becoming Quanta

A. Introduction

This may seem an unlikely place to begin a discussion of Bergson's view of physical reality. The discussions of memory theory, fractal geometry, biological time and psychiatry presented so far certainly do not seem to lead to it. But at least three previous discussions do set the stage for the consideration of physics. One is the account that has been given of Bergson's physical cosmology, an account which portrays his dynamic concepts of the creation and development of the universe. The second is the description of the new nonlinear thermodynamics and Bergson's influence on it. The third is the explanation, just completed, of how Bergson believes it is possible for us to apply mathematics to the world and succeed in doing so--even though that world has a qualitative durational character.

It is hard from our present perspective to understand the mindset of science at the end of the nineteenth century when Bergson was framing his ideas. The general spirit of physicists then was one of security, if not self-satisfaction. The conceptual foundations laid down by Newton at the end of the seventeenth century appeared solid. If anything, they were stronger and more precise than when Newton formulated them originally. But even as scientists celebrated, the eclipse of the old physics was imminent. Only a handful of thinkers suspected it. As we will see, Bergson was one of them.

The two major factors fundamental to the change in physics were the emergence of quantum and relativity. But there were other factors. Prominent among these was the breakdown or fragmentation of the atom. Newton had viewed the atom as a mass particle. Whether or not it was indivisible he did not know. Equally challenging, he was unable to demonstrate how many kinds of mass particles there are. The formulations of the periodic table of the elements by Mendelaev in the 19th century resolved this problem. Now it was possible to show both how many kinds of ultimate particles exist and what are their characteristics. Physics was able to demonstrate not only the nature of the ultimate entities in nature but to classify them in detail.

But almost overnight the assumptions of the prevailing faith in the atom began to fail. Bergson has foreseen the weaknesses in the prevailing concept of the atom. In *Matter and Memory,* he protested that the solidarity and inertia of the atom "...dissolve either into movements or lines of force whose reciprocal solidarity brings us back to universal solidarity."[1] Physics itself was beginning to give up the notion that the atom exists in splendid isolation. If it or its components are one, it is not in the sense of a hard solid unity.

Bergson's protest, however odd it may have appeared to his contemporaries, began immediately to be relevant. In the year in which he published *Matter and Memory,* Jean Becquerel discovered radioactivity. A year later J. J. Thompson discovered the electron. Two years earlier William Roentgen had discovered x-rays. These three discoveries were soon followed by a series of others. Only two years into the twentieth century Lord Rutherford, basing his research on the newly discovered radioactivity, developed his theory of the disintegration of the atom, which was now viewed as a nucleus surrounded by electron orbits. The one, definitively, had become many. Now it was up to quantum physics to explain what the new entities were.[2]

Quantum physics dates from the formulation of Planck's constant in 1900. Closely connected with Rutherford's research on blackbody radiation, it was associated, not without irony, with the Ultraviolet Catastrophe. To the great consternation of physicists, calculations based on the prevailing wave theory showed that all the energy in the universe should by now have radiated away. Only a vast formless mass of waves should now exist.

To escape this dire result, Planck had to give up the prevailing belief that energy is given off in wave-like continuity. Rather, he concluded, it must be given off discontinuously, in packets of energy or "quanta." When matter is thus quantized it no longer radiates energy in unlimited amounts. The universe is thus saved from a formless fate resembling an unending academic committee meeting.

Planck's constant—**6.62607004 x 10^{-34}**—to put it mildly, is a very small number: thirty-four zeroes preceded by a decimal point followed by 10. The equation in which it appears thus deals with the extremely small and the extremely brief. It is **E=hf** where **E** stands for the energy of each quantum of light; **h** for Planck's constant, of course; and f for the frequency of light. When this equation is used, it produces dizzyingly high frequencies. One is no longer in the world of medium-sized objects. One is in a miniscule world where things do not behave as they do in the world of common experience.

---

[1] MM, 200.

[2] For a general account of this history, see Micheal L'Annunziale, *Radioactivity: Introduction and history* (New York: Elsevier, 2007), 632.

Scientists were quick to seize on Planck's achievement, with results that they found surprising. Motion (say, of an electron moving from point A to point B) could no longer be understood as the passage of a solid through an empty space. Rather, it had to be viewed as a successive series of appearances of bundles of energy. Equally challenging: in the early quantum physics, an atom which absorbs or emits photons had to be understood as jumping discontinuously from one energy state to another. Thus, the electrons orbiting the nucleus had to jump from one orbit to the next without passing through the intervening space just as the electron moving from A to Z had to make distinct successive appearances before arriving at Z.

Alfred North Whitehead parodies the un-commonsensical aspects of the new situation in physics very effectively. The new physics, he explains could be understood through a hypothetical railroad trip from Cambridge down to London. In this sixty-mile transit, the train would have to be understood as standing for sixty seconds at each milepost before moving (i.e. jumping) to the next where it would remain for sixty seconds. Similarly for the atoms passage discontinuously from one energy state to the next with the sudden transformation of electron orbits. This, Whitehead points out, would be like a train jumping from one set of tracks to another without passing through the space between them.[3]

This early picture of the motion of quantized particles was changing even as Whitehead wrote about it. The result was the celebrated Copenhagen Interpretation, sometimes termed "Classical Quantum Physics." Completed in 1927 by Niels Bohr, Werner Heisenberg, Max Born and others, it is still subscribed to by the majority of physicists--though it is now subject to increasing criticism.

If the early quantum theory seemed to confound common-sense, the later quantum theory courted paradox. It is not unusual today for physicists to speak of "quantum weirdness." In what follows I will deal with only three examples of this puzzling state of affairs: Helsenberg's uncertainty relations, Bohr's principle of complementarity, and Schrödinger's wave mechanics. This is an abbreviated list. But it will be sufficient to allow us to compare Bergson's physics with its quantum counterpart.

On Heisenberg's terms, though motion is still understood as units of energy following each other in succession, these units no longer make distinct jumps only to halt like Whitehead's phantom train, at an instant. Indeed, it is now instants themselves which cannot be taken for granted. The first formulation of Heisenberg's uncertainty principle is $\Delta x\, \Delta p \geq \hbar$ where x stands for momentum;

---

[3] Alfred North Whitehead, *Science and the Modern World* (New York: The Free Press, 1967), 129-137.

p for position; and, of course, $\hbar$ for Planck's constant. The problem is that while in all prior physics it was assumed that position and momentum could be stated independently and with precision, for Heisenberg if position is stated with perfect precision, momentum becomes infinite. Inversely, if momentum is measured with precision, position becomes indefinite. The best one can do is live with more-or-less position, more-or-less momentum. The second formulation of Heisenberg's relations is $\Delta E \, \Delta t = \hbar$ where **E** is energy and **t** is time.[4]

Here again one is on the horns of a dilemma. If energy is measured perfectly, the time of microevents becomes perfectly indefinite. We have no idea when they take place. Similarly, if we can specify time with accuracy, energy becomes infinite. On either formulation, the precision we expect is impossible to find. We find instead a compromise between inexact alternatives.

A similar two-sided approach is suggested by Niels Bohr's principle of complementarity. Throughout the nineteenth century physicists had debated whether light is a wave or a particle. For Newton it was a particle, for his opponents a wave. Most scientists supported the wave theory. But the nagging question remained. Are we sure the wave theory is correct? Both sides were able to point out phenomena which supported their viewpoint. But no matter what position was taken, it was assumed that eventually one side or the other would be proved correct. There would be wave or there would be particle.

Bohr, working with available experimental procedures, was unconvinced. Diffraction experiments supported the wave theory, experiments with photons (the photoelectric effect, discovered by Einstein) supported the particle theory. But no experiment could decide in favor of one or the other. The result is analogous to Heisenberg's dilemma. One will have a disjunction, in this case not of position or momentum but of wave or particle. One cannot assert either by itself. The result is an inescapable "complementarity": in one experimental context there are waves, in the other particles. No grand experiment can embrace both or decide in favor of either. There is only wave-particle duality: wave *or* particle. All the rest is calculation.

Our third case-in-point is the Schrödinger wave, the central component of the famous Schrödinger equation.[5] The center of contemporary debates on quantum measurement, the Schrödinger equation introduces a concept not seen in previous physics: a wave not of water or air but of probabilities,

---

[4] There are two other formulations (four in all) of Heisenberg's principle. These two concern position and momentum, energy and time, and involve not straight line motion but angular momentum.

[5] Schrödinger provides two formulations of his equation, time-dependent and time-independent. I am dealing here with the former.

specifying all the outcomes that can take place in some given context. The technical term for this coexistence of probabilities is superposition. Take an electron. It can move to any number of positions, some more probable some less so. When a measurement is made, Schrödinger's wave "collapses," giving rise to one actual state. The electron is no longer in many places at once (many probability states or eigenstates) but is here in one state, one position. One has thus gone from an immaterial wave to a particular and exact particle. As the poet, to quote Shakespeare, gives to airy nothingness a local habitation and a name.

The puzzling thing about the Schrödinger wave and its superposition of probabilities is that it seems to allow for the coexistence of contradictory properties. This is shown dramatically by a paper published by Schrödinger in 1935.[6] On the basis of superposition, for example, an atom can exist both in a decayed and undecayed state. Thus, a cat in a sealed container containing ambiguous atoms (decayed and undecayed) cannot be known to be alive or dead if the atomic decay will release a poison that kills the cat. Thus, not just the atom of superposition. The radioactive atom is decayed and undecayed; the cat is both alive or dead: so far as we can tell. The paradox of Schrödinger's cat has sparked a long series of intense debates.[7] It is safe to say that Schrödinger's paradox has not been resolved. It remains at the center of quantum theory.

When Schrödinger devised his wave equation, he assumed that the measurement which occasions the wave's collapse is instantaneous. He did not explain this instantaneity, which remained one of quantum physics' puzzles. Recent experiments, however, have cast doubt on this assumption. On the newer view both the measurement and the collapse of the wave function exhibit the properties of a collapse. The collapse takes time to happen. It is really a process. This is an important conceptual change. Its discoverers believe it will have significant effects on our view of quantum physics.[8]

B. Bergsonian Matter and Quantum Physics: Some Striking Parallels

The account just given of some fundamental features of quantum physics is not intended as either detailed or profound. It is sufficient, as stated above, to allow

---

[6] Erwin Schrödinger, "Die gegenwartige situation in der Quantenmechanik," *Naturwissenschaften* 23, no. 48 (1935): 807-812. For a translation of this essay, see John D. Trimmer, "The Present Situation in Quantum Mechanics. A Translation of Schrödinger 's 'Cat Paradox.'" *Proceedings of the American Philosophical Society* 121, no. 5 (1981): 323-338.

[7] J.A Wheeler and W. H. Zurek, eds., *Quantum Theory and Measurement* (Princeton: Princeton University Press, 1983), 791.

[8] Philip Ball, "Reality in the Making," *New Scientist* 245, no. 3275 (2020): 35-38.

a comparison of Bergson's theory of matter both with the Newtonian theory which preceded it and the quantum theory which was to follow. The results will be surprising. No claim will be made that Bergson "discovered" quantum physics. But, particularly given his reputation as antiscientific, the parallels between his standpoint and that of quantum physics turn out to be striking.

In what follows four of these parallels will be described:

1. Bergson's contention, developed long before Heisenberg's discoveries, that at the microlevel there is real, objective indeterminism.
2. His critique of the entrenched concept of the particle in tandem with his attempts to provide an alternative to it.
3. His belief that what physicist in his time termed "waves" not only require no supplementation but need to be understood as requiring no static support.
4. His quantum-like account of motion as a series of pulses of energy.

The discussion will also include an account of Bergson's response to the new physics, a response which clarifies both his expectation that such a physics would emerge and the general nature of the concepts it would contain. It will also present an account of the physicist Louis de Broglie's essay on Bergson. De Broglie's insights add significantly to the parallels to be discussed in this chapter.

Once again it will help to recall Bergson's concept of temporal hierarchy. At one limit of this hierarchy there is human consciousness with its prolonged rhythms, at the other the extremely brief rhythms of the physical world. As we have seen, he understands the temporal hierarchy as embodying a limit concept: it continues indefinitely towards brevity in time and minuteness in space. At the limit would be the spatial point and the temporal instant. Were this limit ever reached there would be a purely mathematical world consisting of a series of instants.

The point is that for Bergson matter does not reach this limit. If not, then what exists this side of the limit must consist of rhythms of duration, however brief. And if so, matter must contain the fundamental characteristics of duration: continuity, dynamism, and spontaneity. Most of the behavior of matter is predictable. Continuity, spontaneity are reduced to a minimum; but for Bergson, that minimum exists. This is the point he makes in *Matter and Memory* when he states:

> Absolute necessity would be represented by a perfect equivalence of the successive moments of duration, each-to-each. Is it so with the duration of the material universe? Can each moment be mathematically deduced from the preceding moment? We have throughout this work, and for the convenience of study, supposed that it was really so, and such is, in fact,

the distance between the rhythm of our duration and the flow of things, that the contingency of the course of nature, so profoundly studied in recent philosophy, must be practically equivalent to necessity. So let us keep to our hypothesis, though it might have to be attenuated."[9]

That is, he speculates, physics itself might come to support the philosopher's speculation. In this he is agreeing with his teacher Émile Boutroux that the grip of determinism on physical reality is not complete: Boutroux's views are presented in his *The Contingency of the Laws of Nature* (1847) where he argues for a fundamental contingency in the behavior of matter.[10] But he adds something interesting. The fundamental causes in nature (les variations élémentaires) may be so minute that they could not be detected by the measuring instruments available in the nineteenth century. Boutroux then looks to physics itself for the resolution of the question of indeterminacy in matter. Bergson follows him.

Both Bergson and Boutroux, then, suspect that their indeterminist views will be validated by science. It can thus be argued that they are submitting their views to verification, or had things turned out differently, falsification. It appears that the indeterminist view has won out. Attempts by David Bohm and others to find "hidden variables" which reestablish the old determinism have failed. Since deterministic behavior cannot be found in either the equations of quantum physics or in its observations or predictions, most physicists today conclude that at the microlevel one finds indeterminism. That is, if determinism cannot be found by any means, theoretical or experimental, we are likely to conclude that it does not exist. Heisenberg's original uncertainty principle thus becomes a principle not of uncertainty but of spontaneity: of indeterminism. If we cannot find position and momentum or time and energy simultaneously, the determinism represented by that simultaneity does not exist.

It is rare that significant conceptual change--a paradigm shift, to use Kuhn's terminology, transforms only one concept. This is certainly true of quantum physics. Along with the change in the concept of determinism in the new physics comes a change in the notion of the ultimate entities: the particle.

---

[9] MM, 248. Over two decades later, in *The Creative Mind*, he makes exactly the same claim in exactly the same terms, this time citing the advances in physics to support his views. Cf. CM, 303, footnote 6.

[10] Émile Boutroux, *The Contingency of the Laws of Nature*, trans. F. Rothwell (Chicago: Open Court, 1916), 196. Also, *De la contingence des lois de la nature* (Paris: Librairie Germer Bailler, 1874), 152. Bergson may also have been referring to the similar views of Charles Sanders Peirce, "The Doctrine of Necessity Examined," *Monist* 2, no. 3 (1892): 321-337. [This last entry gets reprinted in Vol 5 of *The Collected Papers of C.S. Peirce*.]

The traditional concept of the particle involves solidity or much the same thing, impenetrability. Two physical objects, common sense tells us, cannot be in the same place at one time. But in *Time and Free Will* Bergson attacks this notion, holding that it really amounts to not an assumption about the nature of matter but about the nature of space and number. We think we are adding something to the idea of two or more objects by saying that they cannot occupy the same place. But by asserting that they are *two*, we have already brought in the concept of their complete mutual independence.

> "Hence to assert the impenetrability of matter is simply to recognize the inter-connection between the notions of number and space, it is to state a property of number and not of matter."[11]

Unwittingly we have committed the fallacy of misplaced concreteness: taking our numerical abstractions to be real and treating reality as a (geometrical, mathematical) abstraction. But if this is true, then in realizing it we can move on to consider other, more adequate conceptions of matter, in which some degree of mutual interpenetration can be shown to hold. But then we would have transformed the nature of the particle.

This transformation, as we have seen, has taken place. It is found in Niels Bohr's principle of complementarity, for which particles as such do not exist. Bergson's response to Bohr's wave-particle duality helps us to understand his standpoint. In his final book, a 1934 collection of essays titled *La pensée et le mouvant* (translated as *The Creative Mind*),[12] the philosopher, as we have seen, gives us insights both into the development of his concept of matter and into the agreement of his concept of rhythms of matter with Bohr's "wavicle": the notion of matter as having continuous (wave) and discontinuous (particle) aspects.

In his first work, Bergson tells us, he could do little more than describe matter as "movements of movements."[13] This allowed him to make some sense out of his belief that it is not necessary to find an immobile support for matter, an unchanging foundation for change. In his second book, *Matter and Memory* he was able to move farther, depicting--as we have seen--matter as extraordinarily brief rhythms of duration: "vibrations, perturbations, changes of energy."[14] This could at least point the direction in which physics might go. Finally, in

---

[11] TFW, 39.

[12] Henri Bergson, *La pensée et le mouvant* (Paris: Presses Universitaires de France, 2014), 294.

[13] CM, 84.

[14] MM, 201.

"The Perception of Change,"[15] a talk given at Oxford in 1911, Bergson states, he was able to devote an entire essay to what he believed to be the basic problem: that of replacing the inert particle by some more dynamic notion, possessing activity.[16]

This for him is not a mere metaphysical speculation, in the sense of an empty claim, going nowhere. Sooner or later, he believed, physics would be forced to give up the notion of the particle or corpuscle and replace it with concepts which contain an element of becoming: of duration.[17] To explain his viewpoint Bergson cites a then recent article by Gaston Bachelard, "The Noumenon and Microphysics," in which Bachelard presents an account of the new physics very close to Bergson's.[18]

It is no accident that Bergson should have cited Bachelard's essay. In describing the constituents of the new physics as being dependent on their physical environment, Bachelard intends to include their continuous and dynamic properties. Thus, he writes that in the world of the atom there is,

> ...a sort of fusion between act and being, between the wave and the particle. Must we speak of complementary aspects or complementary realities? Is it not a matter of a more profound cooperation of the object and movement, of a complex energy in which that which is and that which become converge?[19]

No doubt Bachelard was not trying to restate Bergson's position. Even so, he could hardly have stated it more closely. On still another point he concurs with Bergson. That is, he believes, for physics it is no longer a matter of mathematics describing an absolute given reality (i.e. the particle); rather, mathematics defines that reality, is the fundamental means of describing it: "...the fact of being thought mathematically is the mark of an existence at once organic and objective."[20] Clearly this is not the old mathematics. It is a combination, to use Pascal's phrase, of "the spirit of finesse and the spirit of geometry."[21] One has not only a new physics. One has also a new way of thinking.

---

[15] CM, 153-186.

[16] CM, 184.

[17] CM, 185.

[18] Gaston Bachelard, "Noumène et microphysique," *Recherches Philosophiques* 1 (1932): 55-65. (All future references to this work will be cited in the text as NM.)

[19] NM, 56; my translation.

[20] NM, 58; author's translation.

[21] NM, 57.

That is Bergon's opinion. Sooner or later, he tells us, science would be forced to see,

> …in the fixity of the element a form of mobility. When that time came, it is true, science would give up looking for an imagined representation of it, the image of movement being that of a moving point (that is to say, always of a minute solid). In actual fact, the great theoretical discoveries of recent years have led physicists to suppose a kind of fusion between the wave and the corpuscle--between substance and movement, as I should express it.[22]

That is, from the beginning he had believed that something like Bohr's wave-particle duality would arise in physics. But he was not satisfied with the concepts he was able to come up with, thus letting the matter rest.

Bergson says the same thing to the young graduate student Milič Čapek, who in 1938 had sent him a copy of his dissertation stressing the parallels between Bergson's ideas and contemporary physics. He states that his ideas concerning the nature of matter:

> …were formulated when it was regarded as self-evident that the ultimate material elements should be conceived on the image of a (macroscopic) whole, they confused most readers and were most frequently set aside as an unintelligible part of my work. It was probably assumed that it was an unnecessary part.[23]

But, he continues, his view of matter is essential to his philosophy. It is fundamental.

One can easily imagine the philosopher's frustration. Apart from his theory of matter neither his account of perception or his biology, to mention only two components of his philosophy, could be understood. Only the profound mathematician and philosopher Alfred North Whitehead, he tells us, noticed and understood what he was driving at. Yet his theory of duration lay in the direction in which theoretical physics, he believed, would move.[24]

We now come to the third point on which Bergson's approach to physical reality parallels that of quantum physics, his wave concept. The wave concept proposed in nineteenth-century physics may seem a fully dynamic notion. But

---

[22] CM, 85.

[23] Milič Čapek, *Bergson and Modern Physics* (Dordrecht-Holland: D. Reidel, 1971), x-xi, 401. For a full copy of Bergson's letter, "Bergson à M. Capek. July 3, 1938." *Correspondances*, ed. André Robinet (Paris: Presses Universitaires de France, 2002), 1596-7.

[24] BMP, 401.

as understood by scientists a wave could not exist simply as a wave. It was dependent on a subordinate concept, the luminiferous (light-bearing) ether. Just as water waves depend upon water for their propagation, so light waves were thought to depend on the luminiferous ether in order to have something to wave in.[25] When James Clerk Maxwell was able to demonstrate that light is an electromagnetic phenomenon, he felt justified in concluding that both light and electromagnetism required the ether in order to exist.[26] Many physicists at the time, dissatisfied with trying to picture the ether as a peculiar "elastic medium" understood it as a collection of hypothetical ether particles. If so, the prevailing wave theory would have been reduced to a theory about particles.

If for classical nineteenth-century physics waves require a non-wave material support, this is not true of quantum physics. In the words of Robert B. Laughlin:

> ...we accept as nonexistent the medium that moves when waves of quantum mechanics propagate. This is a problem considerably more troublesome than that of light, however, because quantum waves are matter and, moreover, have measurable aspects incompatible with vibrations of a substance.[27]

Quantum physics thus gives up the substance support for waves, which no longer require a subordinate medium in order to exist. The parallel with Bergson is obvious. For him duration at all levels is self-subsistent. It requires no support at any level and can exist in and of itself.

Finally, we come to motion. The classical concept of motion--the transit of a solid particle through an empty space--has at least the virtue of visual clarity. One can easily imagine it and understand it on these terms. But this was from the beginning not Bergson's understanding. For Bergson as for quantum physics the homogeneous persistence of the Newtonian mass particle turns out to be a punctuated existence: a succession of rhythms of duration. For both the philosopher and the scientist neither rest nor motion is a simple persistence through time. It is a succession of becomings, of processes, each following on the other.

---

[25] Since the ether was supposed to be at rest in (immobile) absolute space, there was also a strong tendency to identify it with this timeless Euclidean container.

[26] James Clark Maxwell, *A Treatise on Electricity and Magnetism* (Oxford: Clarendon Press, 1875). Especially Chapter 20, Part IV, "Electromagnetic Theory of Light."

[27] Robert B. Laughlin, *A Different Universe: Reinventing Physics from the Bottom Down* (New York: Basic Books, 2005), 56. Laughlin is a critic of quantum ideas.

C. Louis de Broglie's Bergsonian Essay

The most fundamental feature of Louis de Broglie's essay on Bergson is its acceptance of the Bergsonian problematic: that there is a dramatic contrast between the mobility of things and our mathematical description of them.[28] The arrow in flight moves; our usual representation of its motion pegs it at a point or an instant: static. This, de Broglie believes, constitutes a real problem. It also leads de Broglie to give a Bergsonian interpretation of quantum physics, opposing the static components of the Copenhagen disjunctions to a dynamic context. With regards to Heisenberg, de Broglie states,

> ...it is impossible to know at the same time with precision the dynamic aspect of elementary processes and their spatial localization; and this impossibility is expressed quantitatively by Heisenberg's famous uncertainty relations.[29]

Again, the same contrast is found in Bohr's complementarity:

> What must be said is that an elementary physical entity may be in turn represented through the concept of the particle, that is, as a point precisely located in geometrical space, and by the concept of a wave, which in *wave* mechanics represents motion in a pure state with no spatial location.[30]

Thus, de Broglie continues, for Heisenberg, Bohr and Bergson the fundamental insight is the conflict between mobility and localization, which, in its own terms, quantum physics attempts to overcome.

De Broglie clearly describes the parallel between the Bergsonian and the quantum concept of a wave. A professor of wave mechanics, in explaining quantum waves, would state, according to de Broglie:

> Let us consider a corpuscle animated with a perfectly definite state of motion, that is, corresponding to an exactly known energy and quantity of motion and *let us abstract entirely from the position of the particle in*

---

[28] Louis de Broglie, "The Concepts of Contemporary Physics and Bergson's Ideas on Time and Motion," *Bergson and the Evolution of Physics*, ed. and trans. Pete A.Y. Gunter (Knoxville, TN: University of Tennessee Press, 1969), 45-62. (All future references to this item will be cited in the text as CCP.) De Broglie's essay was first published in *Physique et microphysique*, 1947.

[29] CCP, 53.

[30] CCP, 54.

space: this non-localized state of motion is described in wave-mechanics through the propagation of the plane monochromatic wave.[31]

That is the meaning of de Broglie's phrase "pure state with no spatial location": a non-localized state of motion is what he finds in Bergson's writing when the philosopher, in attempting to distinguish process as such from our spatial representations of it, asks us to fix our attention on these movements by "abstracting from the divisible state that underlies them and considering only their mobility."[32] This allows us to isolate and concentrate our attention on mobility *per se*. We can thus, with some difficulty, understand Bergson's idea of the wave aspect of things.

De Broglie also deals with Bergson's rejection of the assumption that particles (to consider the other half of Bohr's complementarity) are impenetrable, taking it even farther than Bergson did. Bergson had protested against the motion of matter's impenetrability or infinite hardness, leaving open the possibility that the ultimate constituents of matter could overlap or interpenetrate.

Impenetrability as we have seen is for Bergson a mathematical, not a physical concept. De Broglie adds to this protest a further difficulty of wave mechanics, that of numbering the quantum particles. He states:

> ...for particles of the same physical species it is possible to distinguish between them only through their spatial positions, now in wave mechanics one cannot in general attribute to particles well-defined positions in space. If their regions of possible presence merge or overlap--how can one follow their individuality?[33]

The most that can be done is to consider the total number of particles of the same kind, which can be ascertained through further new measurements. One must add to the Nobelist's portrayal of the non-numerability of particles in wave mechanics that for Bergson though numbering (and counting) if they are in some respects problematic, shares the realism of wave mechanics. Rhythms of duration continue to exist as such for him, though the problems of localizing and counting them are, given their nature, quite real.

Our description of de Broglie's account of Bergson's physics from the vantage point of wave theory could end, here. It has covered the basic similarities between the philosopher's insights and those of classical quantum physics as seen by one of its creators. But one more analogy, which de Broglie points out,

---

[31] CCP, 55f.

[32] MM, 276; also, 232.

[33] CCP, 59.

can be helpful. It is that between Bergson's critique of the active and always incomplete character of duration which involves "hesitation" between alternative choices. De Broglie finds an analogous behavior in the quantum concept of matter. The new physics, de Broglie observes, gives up the definite predictions of Newtonian physics, "simple probabilities referring to diverse possibilities."[34] But the outcome of these probabilistic processes is not known beforehand. At each moment they are being worked out. De Broglie describes this continuing process as nature "hesitating between a multitude of possibilities."[35] He notes Bergson's statement in *The Creative Mind* that "time is this very hesitation or it is nothing."[36] We do not often think of time or natural processes in these terms. But it is hard to rule it out once we accept time's incompleteness and its creativity.[37]

This brief survey of de Broglie's account of Bergson's physics provides two useful results. It broadens our knowledge of quantum physics, adding phenomena not originally discussed in this essay, and it deepens our understanding of Bergson's position by showing how these additional factors (numbering, the "choice" of possibles, the nature of quantum waves) can help make sense of his speculations. It would be possible to end this chapter at this point. But I would like to add one more section, on the structure of the duration of matter. If we can understand how duration is configured at the microlevel we can get a still better grasp of what Bergson thinks matter is. This should clarify still farther the relations between his philosophy and quantum physics. It will also prepare us for the next chapter, on Bergson's critique of relativity physics.

D. At the Limit: The Structure of Material Duration

We have been able in this chapter to gain a broad understanding of some main features of quantum mechanics and their relations to Bergson's concepts of matter, motion, particle and wave. This section will add to our understanding not by dealing with physics but by exploring in greater detail the nature of duration at the lower level of his temporal hierarchy: at the limit. This exploration will, I believe, clarify not only the structure of the duration of matter but will help us make sense of the complementarity he finds between the wave and the particle aspects of the ultimate constituents of physical nature. It thus adds to our earlier descriptions of the lower limit of Bergson's temporal hierarchy.

---

[34] CCP, 56.

[35] CCP, 57.

[36] CM, 93.

[37] That Bergson was aware of de Broglie is shown by his comments to Jacques Chevalier. Cf. Jacques Chevalier, *Entretiens avec Bergson* (Paris: Plon, 1949), 255, 296.

It is an interesting fact that in those passages in which Bergson developes his concepts of motion and of matter, he uses many terms to characterize the rhythms of material duration but never the word "wave." This can hardly have been an accident. If he had used it, he would have been readily understood by his readers who were fully aware of the wave concept of prevailing physics. That he did not make use of this readily understood term suggests strongly that from the beginning he had something else in mind.

Fortunately, Bergson has given us a passage which fully clarifies his notion of the temporality of matter. Writing in *Duration and Simultaneity* (1922), he considers the characteristics of matter at the lowest, briefest level. Most importantly, he states; the moments of physical nature, in order to be moments (part of a temporal series) must have some intrinsic connection to the past. This by definition would be memory:

> Without an elementary memory which connects the two moments, there will only be one or the other, consequently a single instant, no before or after, no succession, no time.[38]

As a minimal condition of duration there must be some element of memory, some survival of the past in the present. But in the case of matter our reach is extremely limited: it extends no farther than the immediately prior moment. Along with this minimal duration there will be "...a perpetually new forgetting of what was not in the immediate prior moment."[39] As we have repeatedly stressed, the present state of a physical body depends exclusively not on what happened in the distant past, but on what happened at the previous instant.[40]

This character of material duration can be seen all the more clearly when it is contrasted with that of human consciousness. A passage in *Matter and Memory* dealing with the free act makes this contrast especially vivid. The free act, he insists, does not take place in isolation from our prior experience. It is, rather, a "synthesis of the past and present with a view to the future."[41] But it is not merely the immediate past which is required. The deep past of the individual is organized in the free act:

> ...with the present in a new and richer decision...living with an intenser life, contracting by its memory of the immediate experience a growing

---

[38] DS, 48.

[39] DS, 49.

[40] CE, 13.

[41] MM, 220.

number of external moments...it becomes more capable of creating acts which pass more easily through the meshes of necessity.[42]

The tendency of the free act is thus towards an increasing inclusion of the past, the tendency of physical matter is towards an exclusion of all but the immediately prior moment.

Bergson's treatment of the briefest possible pulse of duration has two important consequences, one for his understanding of temporal, the other of spatial, relationships. The successive moments of matter are for him, if not distinct, then very nearly so. They can be treated as approximating an epochal or temporally atomistic existence, each very nearly independent of its predecessors. The same is true of the spatial relations between microphysical durations. Though none would be entirely independent of its contemporaries (as is the case with a Democritean atom or a Newtonian mass particle), the influence of contemporaries on each other would be, in most contexts, minimal. A good example of this would be the neutrino, millions of which pass through each of us at each moment without, so far as anyone is able to detect, having the least effect on us or each other.

How does this lead us to the wave-particle duality in Bergson's thought? In emphasizing the localized and distinct characteristics of his rhythms of duration he establishes their particle-like character. But in describing them as rhythms he introduces their wave character. The internal activity of the rhythms of matter in tandem with (one might say, in synch with) their transfer of characteristics to their successors--a transfer which from the perspective of their successors constitutes memory--would constitute its wave nature. It is no exaggeration to conclude that from the beginning Bergson worked with the notion of a fundamental duality at the heart of matter between substance and movement as Bergson later put it, or between being and act.

E. Brief Concluding Remarks

Several points are worth making about this treatment of Bergson's relations to quantum physics. The first is that it sheds a vivid light on his philosophical method and its value. Bergson's way of doing philosophy, if it attempts to transcend scientific concepts, also--doubtless paradoxically--attempts to fashion newer concepts which will be more precise and will prove useful. One can say without exaggeration that, certainly in the case of quantum physics he both saw what he perceived to be serious weaknesses in the physics of his time and worked towards a concept of matter space and time which he believed was more accurate and more adequate. The degree to which he succeeded in this is striking.

---

[42] MM, 249.

XIV.

Bergson's Physics:
An Encounter With Relativity

This chapter strikes a very different note from those which preceded it. In the initial chapters of this study, it was shown that Bergson made significant discoveries in the sciences and was able to foresee the outlines of future scientific ideas. But when it came to his approach to relativity physics, things turned out differently. Here Bergson's criticisms of Einstein's physics have been almost universally rejected by the majority of scientists. Bergsonian physics, as I will show, is actually similar to Einstein's in many respects but his failure to refute Einstein made the realization of this affinity seem entirely implausible.

I will divide this chapter into four sections. The first is a general account of relativity physics. There are many ways in which this might be done. I have chosen to do so by way of negation, presenting the "absolutes"— absolute space, place, rest, time, and motion— which were the backbone of Newton's physics. I then show how Einstein's physics can be understood as the systematic denial of each of these. The common sense and Newtonian view that there is a single "now" in which all of us participate and which is present in the entire universe is, for Einstein, false. There are many "nows": as many as there are states of motion. And as for motion, the velocity of a moving object is different when measured from different physical standpoints. Nor is there empty space. Thus, our commonsense world disappears in relativity. A world of fields is what Einstein puts in its place: or rather, a universe consisting of a single space-time field in which individual objects—particles, atoms, speeding rockets—are absorbed.

What is it that Bergson finds so objectionable in this remarkable theory? This will be dealt with in the second section, in which Bergson's criticisms of relativity are focused on Einstein's treatment of time. Temporality, as treated in relativity theory, the French philosopher suggests, scarcely is time at all. It depends on an arbitrary choice of reference systems, having different extents for different and arbitrarily chosen locations. Our experience of life, in the duration experienced by each of us, thus loses its reality. In its place, Einstein offers geometrical measurements which vary according to our choice of standpoints.

Bergson's unrelenting critique of relativity put him at odds with the science community and distanced him from many developments in the physical sciences. But we should not allow this to give rise to a misleading idea of his view of physical reality. We will see shortly that his concept of matter is surprisingly similar in any number of ways to that of quantum physics. In the third section of this chapter, we will see the extent that his notions of matter resemble relativity physics as well. Although a critic of Einstein, Bergson paradoxically was developing notions of the physical world which Einstein himself was working out. The result is a very different picture of Bergson: not as a reactionary thinker who attacked Einstein, but as a thinker who, like the creator of relativity theory, was deeply dissatisfied with the physics of his time and sought ways to transcend it.

Finally, there is the fourth section which discusses the great divide between the two major components of our physics: relativity theory and quantum mechanics. In her *The Physicist and the Philosopher*, Jimena Canales describes the struggle between Einstein and Bergson succinctly: There was a debate, and Bergson lost.[1] One can only agree with her. The public impression left by their debate is one of a triumphant Einstein and a subdued, silent Bergson.

This, however, is not the final word. There is also quantum physics, which cannot be relegated to second place behind relativity. It is, for one thing, our best verified and most useful physics. For another, one searches relativity theory in vain for mention of quarks, leptons, or any member of the subatomic zoo currently organized through the standard model. With regard to the subatomic world, relativity physics is silent. Equally significant, while relativity has only local times and deals with nature deterministically, quantum physics has a single universal time yet views the world in terms of indeterminism. Who then was right: Bergson or Einstein? Since apparently no scientist has a conclusive answer to this question, it remains open.

A. Einstein's Rejection of Newton: New Light

When paradigms shift, as I have stressed, no part changes in isolation. To use a Bergsonian image, the result is kaleidoscopic. A basic conceptual scheme is transformed along with its components and the relations between its components as in a kaleidoscope where a simple twist results in a whole new pattern. In this section I will deal with six of these components: absolute space, place, rest, motion and time, as well as the concept of the particle. Einstein rejects each of these concepts; as we will see, so does Bergson.

---

[1] Jimena Canales, *The Physicist and the Philosopher: Einstein, Bergson, and the Debate that Changed Our Understanding of Time* (Princeton: Princeton University Press, 2015), 450.

For eighteenth and nineteenth century physics, space was little different from the "void" of the ancients: an empty container of all that exists. Newton described it with characteristic brevity:

> Absolute space, in its own nature, without relation to anything external, remains always similar and immovable.[2]

Within this fixture all things move and have their place. Nothing in nature is conceivable without it. As we have seen, this is precisely what Einstein denies. There are for him only the processes of matter. A vast spatial container for matter is needless. There is no one homogeneous timeless thing prior to the goings-on in the world. Einstein is categorical:

> ...we must entirely shun the vague word 'space' of which we must honestly acknowledge, we can not form the slightest conception, and replace it with motion relative to a practically rigid body of reference.[3]

One can conjecture that for Einstein the rejection of space as a fundamental reality marked an important step in his initial investigations.

Once the existence of absolute space is denied, absolute place vanishes with it. Physical objects can no longer be said to have an absolute location in space. They have location only in relation to each other. I am in place in relation to the desk on which I write, and the desk is located in the house in which I live. But both of these are located on planet earth which is located in the solar system which finds its place in our galaxy. There is thus only relative place.

The same argument demolishes the notion of absolute rest. I am at rest relative to my desk and my desk at rest relative to the house in which I live. But both of these are in motion both in relation to the earth's axial spin while the earth revolves in its orbit around the sun. In all this, perfect rest, like perfect location, is nowhere to be found.

This brings us to the 4th absolute, absolute time. In Newton's view, absolute, true, and mathematical time "... of itself and of its own nature flows equably without reference to anything external."[4] The key phrase here is "without reference to anything external." Newton's universal time is transcendent and non-physical. It is more a Platonic entity than a fact of nature. For Einstein, by contrast, the temporal series in nature are found only *in* nature. They are, to use philosophical terminology, immanent not transcendent.

---

[2] Isaac Newton, *Principia Vol. 1. The Motions of Bodies* (Berkeley: University of California Press, 1962), 6. (All future references to this item will be cited in the text as P1)

[3] Albert Einstein, *Relativity. The Special and the General Theory*, 1st ed. (New York: Henry Holt, 1920), 184. (All future references to this item will be cited in the text as R.)

[4] P1, 10.

Finally, there are absolute time and absolute motion, which Einstein eliminates as categorically as he does absolute space, place, and rest. These are replaced by a multitude of local times, each measuring out a rhythm unique to itself and distinct from the others. As we will see shortly, if two things are in motion relative to each other, time is passing at different rates in each. Equally, where for Newton moving objects exist in a common time which makes it possible to measure their absolute velocity, for Einstein the velocity of any object in nature is relative to the place—the "inertial reference system"—from which it is measured. I am thus moving three miles an hour relative to my desk and 30 miles an hour relative to the car driving down the street. Of course, the driver might object that he and his car are in motion while I am stationary. But—and most obviously for velocities near the speed of light—there is no perfectly objective way of making this decision. Motion and time are matters of relative location and of our choice of location.

For common sense relationships such as those about one's desk or for someone in a passing car, this will seem absurd. But there is a factor in such situations which we can easily overlook without making an appreciable error. That factor is light, who's rays make it possible to affirm the existence of ordinary objects in ordinary relationships: that is, to see them. For a physicist like Einstein, however, light cannot be neglected.

To turn again to our two observers, one on a railroad embankment and the other on a passing train, we may think that their watches tick out the same time and that time on the embankment elapses at the same rate on each. But Einstein objects, what will do for common opinion will not do for physics. When the speed of light (184,000 miles per second) is taken into account, we discover that the time of a clock on the train is different from that of one on the embankment. More time passes on the embankment than it does on the train and the clock there is slightly ahead of that on the moving railroad car. These surprising results can be described by a very simple mathematical formulation: if K is the standpoint of the embankment and K' the standpoint of the train,

A clock at rest at the origin x1 = 0 of K, whose beats are characterized by $l = n$, will, when observed from K', have beats characterized by

$$l' = \frac{n}{\sqrt{1 - v^2}}$$

Thus, the clock goes slower at K' than if it were at rest relative to K.[5]

What has been said so far in this section, the reader doubtless realizes, barely sketches relativity physics. It is as much a demonstration of what that theory is

---

[5] Albert Einstein, *The Meaning of Relativity*, 5th ed. (Princeton, NJ: Princeton University Press, 1953), 36f.

not, as a description of what it is. This one sidedness can be in part overcome by taking into account the concepts of field theory on which Einstein relied. If the tendency of 19th century physics was to accept the Newtonian edifice as is, field theory was always an irritant to the majority viewpoint. Could the ideas of field theory, developed by Michael Faraday and James Clerk Maxwell, really be fitted neatly into Newtonian physics? There were doubters, Einstein and Bergson among them. It was entirely surprising to most of the physics community when the doubters prevailed.

We will say more in the third section of this chapter about the field concepts of Faraday and Maxwell in the process of detailing their influence on Bergson. Here, it is enough to define briefly what is meant in physics by a field and to note the extent to which Einstein was dependent on it. *The New World Dictionary* defines a field, as understood in physics, as "a space in which magnetic or electrical lines of force are active." Physicist Lee Smolin defines a field as "physical systems spread out in space…" and also gives electrical and magnetic fields as examples.[6]

Relativity physics, Einstein tells us, makes the notion of field a fundamental— perhaps the most fundamental—concept. This becomes especially evident in his *General Theory of Relativity,* which extends the ideas of relativity to include gravitation. It becomes still more dramatically clear in Einstein's unsuccessful attempt to frame a unified field theory which would contain all possible forces and motions in one majestic view. He was never able to achieve a satisfactory formulation of this theory. But it is clear that he never ceased to believe that the field concept is the most fundamental concept a physicist can use: "The field this becomes an irreducible element of physical description, irreducible in the same sense as the concept of matter in the theory of Newton."[7] Commitment to a field theory with its absolute stress on continuity has many significant implications. One is particularly striking: the elimination from physics of the idea of material particles. Einstein's friend and collaborator, Leopold Infeld, makes this very clear. To someone who objects that we cannot give up the idea of a particle, relativity physics replies:

> The existence of what is known as matter should be deduced from the field equations alone. What is regarded as matter situated in regions in which the field is especially strong.[8]

---

[6] Lee Smolin, *Einstein's Unfinished Revolution* (New York: Penguin Press, 2019), 299.

[7] R, 150.

[8] Leopold Infeld, *Albert Einstein* (New York: Charles Scribner's Sons, 1959), 117. Revised edition.

A resting electron on this view (or, to bring us up to date, a quark) is a small region inside which the field is very strong. It is more accurately understood as concentrated energy. This way Einstein was able, as he put it, "to replace the idea of the material particle (material point) once and for all."[9]

Instant picture of things is thus as far removed from that of Democritus or of Epicurus as it is from Newton. We should look for its analog in the metaphysics of Spinoza, a philosopher cited by Einstein late in his career when he had abandoned the positivism of his early years. In Spinoza as in Einstein, particles become an aspect of the One: a single reality which captures reality in terms of finite modes.

Relativity theory thus gives us a description of the universe dramatically different from that of Newton. In the new view, individual physical things (particles, people, planets) disappear and are absorbed in a single overarching reality: a single entity termed space-time. In this physical monism the solid physical objects we take for granted in our daily lives become aspects of a single field defined in terms of spatial, geometrical relationships. Here time slows down or speeds up according to the motion of physical bodies (so much for an ordinary wristwatch). Equally striking is another phenomenon which is involved in the first, but which like the corresponding time effect, I bring up only now: moving objects in relativity theory contract in the direction of motion. This effect only becomes significant near the speed of light. When one deals with rockets or stellar objects with high velocities, the effect becomes appreciable. It is necessary to point out that the slowing down of time and the diminishing of length in relativity are really one phenomenon, not two. They constitute a single transformation of the prevailing space-time.

What follows from all of this is striking. Though Einstein's universe consists of the ceaseless transformations of space-time in a constant changing of geometrical relations, in the end Einstein declares that the real, the physical world, is timeless. Such a view is rarely stressed or even suggested in Einstein's popular writings. But from Einstein's viewpoint reality is "space-like"[10] rather than time-like. It is also deterministic without exception: what appears to be a future event of uncertain character is known now through its predictability. The picture of space-time which Einstein presents in his books is dynamic: A panorama of incessant transformation with no underlying static or stable framework to reassure us. But this was not his basic view. It is not surprising that shortly before his death in a letter to his friend Michael Besso, Einstein

---

[9] R, 143-151.

[10] R, 141-145.

concluded that though things may seem to change, in reality time is an illusion: nothing but an illusion, which human beings will simply have to accept.

The author is well aware that this outline or sketch of relativity physics as he has said, is incomplete in any number of ways. Its aim, however, is not so much to provide a synoptic vision of Einstein's theory but to present enough information to make an effective discussion of Bergson's approach to relativity possible. He hopes that he has succeeded in this. Fortunately, the discussion of the Bergsonian critique of Einstein in the next section will provide enough additional information to make the fundamentals of relativity clearer to the reader.

B. Bergson's Critique of Relativity: The Paradox of the Twins

As noted above, Bergson's criticisms of relativity are presented in *Duration and Simultaneity*, published in 1921. To simplify his ideas, I will concentrate on the examples cited above: the standpoint of the embankment and the train passing on the tracks. Bergson replaces the embankment and a train with two rockets: One is at rest on the earth; the other is in motion in space. The rocket on the earth contains a gentleman named Peter; the rocket in space, his twin brother, Paul.

If we assume the viewpoint of the special theory of relativity, then a rather odd state of affairs follows. If one of two twins remains earthbound while the other departs on a rocket moving at a velocity close to that of light, the earthbound twin will age at a normal rate while the travelling twin will age far more slowly. On his return he will discover that his earthbound twin has already died while he is only middle aged. One twin may be 200 years old by his brother's calendar and 65 by his own.[11]

Whether we are dealing with trains, rockets, or any other moving object, is this a reality? Or is it a sleight of hand, a mathematical illusion? Bergson thought it was an illusion, created by a spatialization of time and motion. He had two reasons for making this claim. The first, based on the Principle of Relativity, is the assumption that if two systems are in uniform straight line motion relative to each other it is impossible to distinguish which is in motion, which is at rest.[12] Einstein, as we have seen, uses the example of a train moving uniformly in relation to its tracks. If we choose the train as our system of reference, the tracks and the embankment on which they rest are unmoving and the train is

---

[11] Bertrand Russel quips that this will confer an unfair advantage on the moving twin, whose cigar will last much longer than that of the stationary brother. Cf. *The ABC of Relativity* (London: Allen & Unwin, 1962), 54.

[12] R, 12-15.

in motion. If the train is taken as a reference system, the tracks and embankment are in motion and the train is at rest.[13]

This procedure may seem a bit arbitrary. But the results, if the equations of the special theory of relativity are taken into account, are easy to construe as paradoxical, even contradictory. The equations involve a contraction of the moving system in the direction of motion and a slowing down of time. One result, as we have seen, is the differential aging of the two twins. The other is that whether it is measured from the point of view of the embankment or the train, the speed of light is constant. The velocity of the train (or the tracks) may vary, as much as we like. The speed of light will never vary. Another result concerns simultaneity. We are used to the idea that there is a single "now" for the entire universe, a universal simultaneity. In relativity physics this is no longer the case. To continue with the example of the train and the tracks,[14] if we assume two points equidistant from a single point on the tracks (say, at a railroad terminal), points which are also equidistant from the two ends of the train,[15] observers on the train will see two flashes of lighting (or other light signals) which are simultaneous from the vantage point of the embankment but are not simultaneous from the vantage point of the train: "Events which are simultaneous with respect to the embankment are not simultaneous with respect to the train and vice versa (relativity of simultaneity)."[16] *Now* turns out to be *not* a *universal* but a *local* phenomenon: different depending on what we choose to make our reference system; relative to the point from which we make our observations and measurements.

The problem for Bergson is that if one can take either the train or the track, the rocket or planet earth, as an inertial reference system, one can impute the slowing down of time with equal right either to the observers on the train/plane or to those on the embankment-track/earth. In his *Relativity: The Special and The General Theory*, this is certainly how Einstein describes the situation.[17] And even had he expressed himself differently, the theory of relativity is based, as Einstein explains,[18] on the principle of relativity for which the existence of a

---

[13] R, 17-20.

[14] R, 25-7.

[15] In case I'm not being clear about this: the two points equidistant from a common point on the train correspond to the two points equidistant from a common point on the embankment. The light signals coming from these two pairs of points are for relativity physics not in synch.

[16] R, 26.

[17] Bergson refers to this book several times in *Duration and Simultaneity*: 93f, 172, 186.

[18] R, 12-15.

preferred inertial system is *streng verboten.* The two twins are on exactly equal footing.[19]

Hence, we can understand Bergson's claim: the observer on the train in motion does not experience a temporality which differs from that of the observer stationary on the embankment. Naming the observer on the embankment Peter and the observer on the train Paul, he concludes,

> Peter, really motionless, lives a certain duration; Paul, in motion, lives a slower duration. But the other, that of reciprocity, implies that the slower duration must be attributed by Peter to Paul or by Paul to Peter depending on whether Peter or Paul is referrer or referent.[20]

Their durations, in fact, are identical. They live one and the same time but attribute different temporalities to each other. Einstein is wrong. There are no two relative times. There is, for the universe and for the two brothers, one flowing universal time.

This account of Bergson's critique of relativity physics leaves a lot unsaid. For one, it scarcely does justice to his detailed, point-by-point analysis of the relations between the mathematics of relativity and the experience of the observer. For another, it leaves out the debate which followed the publication of his book as well as the literature devoted to its interpretation. One can only hope that enough has been said to make clear the general outlines of Bergson's position and the basics of his critique of relativity physics.

It can be argued that facts have resolved the question of the aging of the twins. Continuing experiments with ions, subatomic particles and radioactive substances are taken by many scientists to have resolved the question. One twin (or one radioactive substance) ages, the other does not. The author has problems with the prevailing interpretation of these experiments. But even if he did not, problems with the relations between relativity and quantum physics raise serious questions about the nature of time. These will be dealt with in the next section.

C. Selected Affinities: The Convergence of Bergson's Physics and Einstein's

If Bergson is known simply as an opponent of Einstein, that is unfortunate. Surprisingly, in the years from the publication of *Matter and Memory* (1896) and *Creative Evolution* (1907), he was developing concepts of physical nature

---

[19] See Herbert Dingle's introduction to the English translation of *Duration and Simultaneity* (xv-xlii) for a discussion of these points. Dingle was one of the few philosophers of science who agreed with Bergson.

[20] DS, 77.

very much at odds with Newton and the Newtonians. These were largely submerged in the text of his books; thusly, moreover, ignored by his contemporaries. But it is possible to single them out and describe their convergence with Einstein's viewpoint. We might say (using a catchy phrase) that Bergson was a semi-Einsteinian anti-Einsteinian. The phrase no doubt is glib. But it makes the point.

Bergson's treatment of space is highly complex. To treat it in depth would require an account not only of its relations to physics but also its relations to his theory of knowledge and theory of perception. That is not necessary here where the basic point is straightforward: Space, he tells us, is not something we can assume as a part of nature. It is a diagram[21] or a symbol[22] by which we navigate the world around us. It helps us to bring order into nature. One is reminded here of Immanuel Kant's account of space as a form of perception. But we have already seen that this cannot be accepted at face value, as a claim that space is simply subjective. We have seen that for Bergson all objects in the world have some degree of spatiality and, in contradiction with views presented in *Time and Free Will*, nothing that exists is simply unextended. Spatiality ("extensity") is present everywhere. But it is clear that pure space—Newton's absolute space—is for Bergson not a reality. The same holds for the concept of "absolute positions in absolute space" as Newton believes,[23] along with, for example Leonhard Euler. [24]

Nothing, then, can be said to be absolutely at rest. One looks in vain for an unmoving part of nature. It would, if it existed, have to be found in space. But space and place, he argues, cannot be found to exist. Nonetheless, if absolute space, place, and rest are banished from the external world, then where is there a place for absolute motion or absolute time?

Bergson is very clear on the subject of absolute motion, whose existence he denies. In an extended discussion in *Matter and Memory*, he asks how absolute motion can be measured. It cannot be derived, as physicist then believed, from "absolute position in absolute space.[25]" These cannot be found. Nor can it be derived from concepts of force[26] which only lead back to the concept of

---

[21] MM, 187, 211, 310.

[22] MM, 219.

[23] MM, 194f.

[24] Leonard Euler, *Theoria motus corporum solidurum seu rigidorum* (Rostochii et Gryphiswaldiea: Litteris et impensis A. F. Rose, 1765), 30-33. Website: https://ecommons.cornell.edu/handle/1813/57675 Accessed 10 Feb 2022.

[25] MM, 194.

[26] MM, 195.

absolute space that one is seeking to avoid. What is given, Bergson argues, is a fundamental, irreducible datum. We confront a world which is a whole: a world in constant change in which motion cannot be referred to bodies with either absolute motion or absolute position.[27] A "moving continuity"[28] is for him all we can find in nature: a world in which things change in relation to each other and move in relation to each other.

Finally, there is absolute time: Newton's perfect universal clock, which ticks with perfect order and which imposes a universal "now," a perfect simultaneity valid for the entire universe. There is no question that Bergson defends the existence of a universal time. It is worthwhile to note, however, that it is not Newton's universal time which he is defending. As we have seen, Newton's absolutes are transcendent, essentially Platonic entities. But for the French philosopher, universal time is found in nature, where it is thoroughly immanent. As Elie During shows, its reality is established by him through empirical measures, by extending the simultaneity found in our local surroundings step by step to the farthest reaches of the universe.[29]

The situation here is complex. In likening Bergson's views to Einstein's, there is no attempt to argue that they are identical. One only wishes to show that for both whatever times that there are, are imminent: found only in nature and established by empirical means. Also, though one might argue that for both Thinkers there are a multiplicity of local times period but Einstein's local times and Bergson's plurality of local durations are quite different sorts of things. Einstein's local times are in no way hierarchically arranged. They share geometrical nonhierarchical relations to each other.[30]

Finally, though I have so far attempted to show the unsuspected similarities between the Einsteinian and the Bergsonian physics, by kind of *via negativa*— an account of their ideas based on what they both denied—there is another approach which needs to be added: an approach which shows still another convergence of their views. This will involve revealing the joint dependence of

---

[27] MM, 196.

[28] MM, 197.

[29] Ellie During, "Temps réel, temps universal, temps cosmolgique: Trois diménsions de la cosmologie Bergonienne," in *Toute ouverte*, eds. S. Abiku, H. Fujita, and M. Goda (New York: Olms, 2019), 99-131. Cf. also During's *Einstein et Bergson: La querelle du temps* (Paris: Presses Universitaires de France, 2016), 368.

[30] It will also help to point out here a problem involving Bergson's terminology. When he describes the motion we find in the world to be "absolute," he means by this to refer to motion as real as opposed to merely a matter of abstract relations. Cf. "An Introduction to Metaphysics" in *The Creative Mind*, trans. M. Andison (New York: The Philosophical Library, 1946), 187-237; especially 227-228.

the two thinkers on the field concept as developed by 19th century electromagnetic theorists.

It is no accident that in *Matter and Memory*, in his prolonged analysis and criticism of the physics of his time, Bergson cites with approval the work of Michael Faraday[31] and James-Clerk Maxwell,[32] two scientists who brought field theory into physics. Of the articles that Bergson cites by Maxwell one is particularly interesting: "On Action at a Distance," read at the Royal Institute of Great Britain in 1873. It is a criticism of Newton's theory of gravity.[33] According to Newton if a massive object were created at time t, its gravitational attraction would be felt instantaneously throughout the universe. This attraction does not take time to cross astronomical distances. Its creation is simultaneous with its being present everywhere at once. Arguing on the basis of electromagnetic theory, Maxwell insists instead that forces in nature must be understood as acting not instantaneously across empty space but successively, through the agency of a field. This should hold not only for electromagnetic lines of force but for all forces.

One finds Maxwell's plurality of active forces again in Bergson's account of the behavior of matter. Matter, Bergson reiterates, is continuous.[34] It consists in the "reciprocal action" of its contents.[35] He speculates that there is no part of matter that does not act on any other.[36] That is, while in dealing with the rhythms of matter at the level of the very small and brief he describes successions of pulses of energy, at the macro-level of the very large and distantly related he describes matter as being a whole, a single dynamic interaction no part of which is without active relations with every other. Motion relative to any body whatever must be reduced to the behavior of a field.

The end result of Bergson's reflections on the nature of matter is not at all what we might expect. If we had imagined that his picture of matter is simply opposed to Einstein's we are in for a surprise. The two thinkers, profoundly influenced by the field concept, agree in rejecting any conceptual superstructure comprised of absolutes. In place of absolute space, motion and rest we find relative rest, motion, and space, comprised only of the relations between its components. The result is for both Bergson and Einstein a universe of constantly interacting

---

[31] MM, 38, 200-201, 259. Also, CE, 131.

[32] MM, 258-9.

[33] James Clerk-Maxwell, "On Action at a Distance," in *The Scientific Papers of James Clerk-Maxwell*, Vol. LIV (Cambridge: Cambridge University Press, 2013), 311-323.

[34] MM, 108, 196, 197, 203, 208, 209, 219, 231; CE 10, 122, 131, 235.

[35] MM, 200, 209, 220.

[36] CE, 130.

patterns, of endless mutual variations in which the shape of things constantly varies and yet the basic physical reality remains. One cannot stress this point too strongly. In dealing with matter in the large the two thinkers, however different in their approach to time and mobility, converge in their picture of physical reality as a single field-like entity, constantly shifting its components. The reality for both is the opposite of a complex of substantial, solid entities. It is that of the constant interaction not of physical substances but of matter conceived as continuously interrelated.

To repeat myself, this is far from the picture of Bergson as a conservative attempting to block the advances of human reason with contrived arguments. His goal from the beginning is not a restatement, much less a defense, of the physics of his time. His outlook, like his method, is focused on a future of conceptual creativity. Thus, we can make sense of his pro-Einstein comments in the preface to *Duration and Simultaneity*. In stating his admiration for the physicist, he sees Einstein has accomplished as deriving from "an intuition of genius, read in Lorentz's equations."[37] We do not have to point out that for Bergson an intuition is a contact with duration. This seems contradictory if the argument of *Duration and Simultaneity* is to be a protest against Einstein's entire physics. But we have seen that this is only a partial view of the French philosopher's standpoint. Einstein for him has effectively critiqued and surpassed static "absolutes" which, Bergson believes, have blocked the way to a truer picture of reality and created "new ways of thinking"[38] which will prove more adequate than their predecessors. A dynamic interpretation of relativity physics is at the basis of both Bergson's appreciation of and his critique of Einstein's achievement.

D. A Dispute Without a Victory: Contradictions in Contemporary Physics

In the early 20th century, many prevailing criticisms of relativity physics were put to rest. Einstein's views were considered validly established: on the graves of those doubting Thomases' who could not be brought to think so. I think it's fair to say, however, that this resolution of doubts can no longer be accepted at face value. Rather than resting on a stable consensus, physics today is divided into two approaches, each of which appears valid from its own viewpoint; neither of which can be viewed as consistent with each other. Put succinctly: where relativity theory presumes a multitude of times relative to the place from which measurements are taken, quantum physics presumes a single universal time valid for all measurements. There are many other differences: Quantum clocks are thus in conflict with relativistic clocks; relativity space, it turns out,

---

[37] DS, 5.

[38] DS, 5.

in contradiction with quantum space. Efforts to resolve the contradictions have been many and brilliant: Nonetheless, so far none has managed to bridge the gap. To this writer, the difficulty is analogous to trying to build a suspension bridge across the Grand Canyon. It would certainly be a heroic feat: but no one has imagined how to do it.

If this is so, then accounts of victory or defeat in the Einstein-Bergson debate, or of yet other debates on the record (one thinks of Einstein's and Bohr's long-continued arguments) need to be revised. As things now stand, there is no final and conclusive way to establish whether the German physicist or the French philosopher is either victor or vanquished. Both concepts of time appear to be equally valid and with them contrasting theories of causality, space, and matter. The author, raised on the assumption that physics is both one and certain, finds this dualism at the heart of science to be all but unbelievable. But it is real, and he finds himself obliged to believe it. To show that Bergson's views are arguably false in relativity physics and in generality true for quantum physics is to leave oneself impaled on the horns of a dilemma.

There is another problem connected with the first and relating to the time of relativity. I find myself unable to resolve it and simply state it as a personal puzzle or quandary. It concerns an axiom which is at the basis of Einstein's concept of reality: the principle of relativity. According to this principle, as we have seen, a body may be considered either at rest or in motion depending on our choice of inertial reference system. A number of recent experiments have shown that the time of a single atom or subatomic particle (that is, "particle") varies in relation to the earth (or, if one wishes, the rest of the physical universe). A mu-meson, for example, has a slowed time if it is in motion in relation to the earth. [39] Therefore, the time dilation predicted by relativity is valid. It is real.

The problem is that on the terms of the principle of relativity—which Einstein came to refer to as the "principle of equivalence"[40]—our decision as to what is in motion or what is not in motion is perfectly arbitrary. We could at a pinch

[39] For example, D.H. Frish and J.H. Smith, "Measurement of the Relativistic Time Dilation using M-Mesons," *American Journal of Physics* 31, no. 5 (1963): 342-355; J.C. Hafele and R.E. Keating, "Around the World Atomic Clocks Predicted Relativistic Time Gains," *Science* 177, no. 4044 (1972): 166-8; H. Bailey et al., "Relativistic Time Dilation for Positive and Negative Muons in a Circular Orbit," *Nature* 268, no. 5516 (1977): 301-35; Dirk Schwalm et al., "Test of time Dilation Using Stored Li+ Ions as Clocks at Relativistic Speeds," *Physical Review Letters* 113 (September 4, 2014). For further confirming experiments see, "Experimental Testing of Time Dilation," *Wikipedia*, https://en.wikipedia.org/wiki/Time_dilation. Accessed 10 Feb 2022.

[40] R, 10; EP, 343.

decide to render the earth in motion and the mu-meson or the atom carried around the earth on an airplane as unmoving. Probably we would be told that this is absurd. The meson or the airliner obviously are moving. The earth, much less the remainder of the universe, are not. But according to the principle of relativity, or equivalence, either view can be assumed. Like the example of the car moving down the street, we can on relativistic grounds declare either the car or our house to be in motion. In the case of the mu-meson, we can decree that the time of the meson slows down, or we can decree its mobility to be real, in which case we can slow down the time of the rest of the universe. This seems absurd. Can we change the time *of the entire universe* by a decision as to whether we will take the cosmos to be an inertial reference system? The principle of equivalence states that we can. But perhaps we will have to doubt the validity of the principle.

Such discussions could be explored with profit in greater depth. I would like to cut them short here by drawing attention to a recent article in *The New Scientist*. The article, by Miriam Frankel, describes an attempt initiated by the Austrian physicists Paul Erker and Marcus Huber to bridge yet another gap in the physical sciences: that between quantum physics and thermodynamics.[41] We recall thermodynamics through the discussion of its reformulation by Ilya Prigogene. According to the second law of thermodynamics, the utilization of energy, which takes place constantly throughout physical nature, gives rise to increasing disorder and hints to an arrow of time. We move exclusively towards the future; although in classical quantum physics, this is not true. For quantum physics equations are reversible, pointing us with equal reality to either the future or the past. Erker and Huber argue, by contrast, that a careful study of clocks—whether an ordinary mechanical clock or the rhythm of a cesium atom—requires an input of energy in order to function. Hence, clocks when accurately understood point to the irreversibility and thus the reality of time. Wherever there is anything clock-like, there is a constant and inescapable upthrust of time towards the future, but never the past. The argument is more complex than this account of the new physics makes it appear. It was shown by the Austrian physicists using clocks constructed simply of atoms, that the more energy is dissipated then the more accurate measurements are. Later experiments in England showed that clocks become more accurate as more energy is used:

> This was the first result to explain why clocks move forward in time, because as they measure time they increase entropy, and irreversible process.[42]

---

[41] Miriam Frankel, "Clock Watchers," *The New Scientist* 253, no. 3367 (January 1, 2022): 46-49. (All further references to this item will be cited in the text as CW.)

[42] CW, 48.

By interrelating quantum physics and thermodynamics, we thus discover a real temporality at the base of things.

Frankel, however, makes a serious mistake, one which, from the viewpoint of this book, is highly instructive. Over a century ago, she notes, two great minds, Bergson and Einstein, clashed over the nature of time. Bergson thought there was more to time than could be explained by clocks, captured by mathematics, or elucidated by psychology. Einstein, by contrast, held that time is a physical entity in a static reality which has been termed the "bloc universe" which lacks a clear past, present, or future. In the new physics, Einstein triumphs, for consciousness is seen, against Bergson, to be a physical entity.

In fact, the author misses the very point that she has made. The fundamental dispute between the scientist and the philosopher is over whether time is real or merely an illusion. The new chronometric interpretation, she shows, makes time (or process or duration) an inescapable reality. It is not Einstein, if this is true, who has won the centuries old debate. It is Bergson.

Whether, however, Bergson must concede that the very real time of clocks is simply physical—doubtless at the expense of psychological duration—is not clear. There are many levels of duration, he states, physical duration being only one of them. But there is a biological time. And there are social and individual human times as well. These intermediate times do not appear to be adequately accounted for in *Duration and Simultaneity*. The question of the reality of human duration, for one, hardly appears to be resolved.

A Realm of New Possibilities: The Nonlinear Thermodynamics of Jeremy English

A. Entropy Production as the Basis for Life

The diverse developments of Bergsonian intuition considered in this book, though they continue to have repercussions in the present, are achievements occurring in the past. In concluding, I would like to give an account of the views of Jeremy England, an American physicist, views which many believe will have important consequences. Though England's theories are in no way indebted to or involved with Bergson's (save indirectly through Prigogine) they fit in well with Bergson's philosophy. It is thus possible to end on a positive note.

Fortunately, our previous account of Ilya Prigogine's work has paved the way for an understanding of England's ideas, which are a reformulation and precising of what Prigogine had been able to accomplish earlier. For classical thermodynamics—thermodynamics through most of history—the production of entropy was strictly linked to the production of disorder. So closely were the concepts of entropy and disorder held together that, we recall, Belousov could not get his paper published describing the new chemical reaction he had discovered. The clocklike regularity and complex scroll of waves were forms of dynamic order, in no way resembling the fate of the burnt match. Prigogine's achievement was to show that the creation of dynamic form is a relatively common phenomenon in nature and to provide a nonlinear mathematics to describe it.

Prigogine's insights made possible a new approach to the emergence--as he termed it—of "order out of chaos." It had important implications for the nature of biological evolution, the functioning of organisms, and the emergence of life itself-- a topic which he returned to throughout his career. But chemical processes far from equilibrium are hard to describe with accuracy. The promise of Prigogine's discoveries thus was blocked by an inability to make precise predictions. More needed to be known about the details of entropy production and the behavior of dissipative structures.

Many of these difficulties were resolved in 1999 by an English scientist, Gavin Crooks, who showed that it was possible to deal in great precision with Prigogine's chemical reactions.[1] For Crooks the entropy process corresponds to a simple ratio between:

1.   the probability that atoms will undergo an entropic process (the striking of a match, the cooling of the cup of coffee)
2.   divided by the probability of the reverse process

As entropy production increases, so does the ratio between 1 and 2. Hence a system's behavior becomes more and more irreversible: predictably so. Crooks was able for the first time to describe microscopic irreversibility in a single equation. In the words of Allison Eck:

> Crooks showed that a group of atoms could similarly take a burst of external energy and use it to transform itself into a new configuration...if the atoms dissipate the energy while they transform, the change could be irreversible. They could always use the next burst of energy that comes along to transform back, and often they will. But sometimes they won't. Sometimes they will use that next burst to transition to yet another new state.[2]

Crooks's results, which link irreversibility and the emergence of new chemical structures of great complexity, portray the opposite. With the dissipation of energy and the consequent production of greater amounts of entropy, new, often dynamic forms emerge.

Crooks's paper was particularly intriguing to England, then a young professor at M.I.T.[3] England had long been interested in problems of biological form and especially in the puzzle of the emergence of life.[4] It was clear to him from Crooks's work that in order to attain the degree of irreversibility and of chemical exuberance that is the hallmark of life, a system would have to be extremely good at absorbing and dissipating heat. But something more was needed. Somehow, given an energy source some arrangement of atoms will be better at absorbing and expending heat than others. Once the situations that efficiently absorb energy in gross amounts and expend it with equal force can be identified, the way would be open to an understanding of the emergence of any

---

[1] Gavin Crooks, "Entropy Production Fluctuation and the Nonequilibrium Work Relation for Free Energy Differences," *Physical Review E* G0 (1999): 2721.

[2] Allison Eck, "How do You Say "Life" in Physics? A New Theory Which Sheds Light on the Emergence of Life's Complexity," *Nautilus* (July 10, 2017), 11 pages. http://nautil.us/issue/50/emergence/how-do-you-say-lifeinphysics-rp. This article was originally published in *Adaptation,* March 2016. (All future references to this item will be cited in the text as HSL.)

[3] England is currently a Principal Research Scientist at the Georgia Institute of Technology.

[4] HSL, 2-3.

number of the components of living things, from the small to the large, extending to the most complex, reaching hopefully to the most elusive of things: the first living cell.

In attempting to explain the origin of life, England involved himself in a difficult problem; one with many possible solutions and as yet no one satisfactory answer. The writer remembers (He was in high school at the time) the dramatic 1952 Miller-Urey experiment which, by launching electrical sparks into a mixture of methane, ammonia, hydrogen and water vapor, produced a number of amino acids: fundamental chemical building blocks of life.[5] The question of the origin of life then appeared to be on the verge of being answered once and for all. But it was not to be. Variations of the Miller-Urey experiment failed to produce the chemicals known to be essential to living things. The result, rather than a solution to the problem, was a proliferation of theories of many kinds. One possibility was that life emerged through the function of certain clays as templates, or through the agency of superheated deep-sea vents, in a thin layer of ice covering the oceans. There were "metabolism first" and "genes first" theories. On the terms of "panspermia" life journeyed to earth from elsewhere in the universe and was not generated on our planet. Many scientists believed that the emergence of life in the universe is simply a fluke: something so improbable that it never should have happened. Yet it did.

For England, there was no need to be pessimistic. From the viewpoint of his theory of dissipative structures, highly complex chemical structures should be seen emerging everywhere. Surely this behavior is an indication of nature's productive capacity. Amino acids, proteins and enzymes were now seen to be emerging more easily than had ever been believed. And if proteins and enzymes, why not life itself?

In 2013, while in California giving a talk at Caltech, England mulled over Crooks's results. To achieve the kind of irreversibility that is the sign of life, he concluded, a system would have to be very good at absorbing and dissipating heat. Crooks had provided an equation which portrayed the conditions under which this can occur. What more was necessary? The answer finally became clear. Assuming a source of energy, some systems will be better at absorbing energy and generating entropy than others. These will generate the new highly complex forms that systems near equilibrium cannot hope to produce. England termed this process dissipation-driven adaptation. From the vantage point of dissipative adaptation, the dissipative process explores possible biological form: a wide array of shapes, any of which can aid the organism to profit from

---

[5] Noam Lahav, *Biogenesis: Theories of Life's Origin* (New York: Oxford University Press, 1998), 340.

its context. The end result could be a transformed organism: possibly a new species.[6]

It is fascinating to follow England's account of the interplay between energy sources (sometimes called "forcing landscapes") and their targets ("chemical reaction networks"). More is involved than the simple expenditure of energy. Energy turns out to be transmitted in specific frequencies or rhythms: a significant case of chemical (not yet biological) time. The response, ie., the network's reaction, is also temporally structured. That is, it "resonates" in response. Its self-restructuring, so as to be able to appropriate ever larger supplies of energy, involves a temporality corresponding to that of its environment. The result is what England describes as "fine tuning": a close and active correspondence in which there are chemical structures that are increasingly able to absorb and dissipate energy. England states straightforwardly:

> By getting continually pushed and knocked around by patterns in the environment, matter can undergo continual exploration of the space of possible shapes whose rhythm and form became matched to those patterns in ways that look an awful lot like living.[7]

Continual forcing by the environment thus leads through perpetual exploration to the emergence of complex form.

This approach, if it is extremely promising, involves its author in a dilemma. For one, if England's approach is highly theoretical, any proof of his theory has to be experimental. This is no easy order. While the confirmation of some theories may consist of simple observational reports (think of Galileo's account of the Moons of Jupiter), by contrast any justification of England's theory must involve chemical experiments of many kinds and of high complexity. This difficulty is accompanied by another: an admitted uncertainty about just which factors are involved in the emergence of life. England admits straightforwardly that he "…does not know anything about how the package deal we call life first gets bundled together."[8]

---

[6] Jeremy England, "Statistical Physics of Self Replication," *Journal of Chemical Physics* 139, no. 121923 (August 2013).

[7] Jeremy England, *Every Life is on Fire: How Thermodynamics Explains the Origins of Living Things* (New York: Basic Books, 2020), 4. (All future references to this item will be cited in the text as LF.)

[8] Brian Clegg, "The Origin of Life: A New Theory Suggests Physics has the Answer," *BBC Focus Magazine* 322 (October 25, 2019). (Future references to this item will be cited in the text as OL.)

But he has good reason to think that his experiments (which for simplicity's sake are performed on a computer) will bring us closer to an answer.

The term "package deal" is apt. Physicists admit that they cannot agree on a satisfactory definition of "life." But most agree that the "package" which defines life must consist of at least three factors: 1. Metabolism; 2. unity, usually understood through the cell membrane; and 3. self-replication. The theory of dissipative adaptation certainly deals with the first of these. England's breakthrough article (cited above) in which he presents his theory and the mathematics which instantiates it, deals with replications. But how the first living cell emerged or even the conditions under which it did so, remain for now unknown.

Even so, there are innumerable processes that England and his colleagues can point to to establish the reality of dissipation-induced form. As Prigogine and his colleagues discovered, finely tuned low-entropy states of driven matter "spring up all over the place."9 Dissipative structures are omnipresent in nature, from turbulent fluids to vibrating crystals. The problem for adaptive dissipation theorists is to choose the examples which converge on a process that can generate life or add insight to the complexities of evolution. The difficulty is not that of a poverty of examples but of an *embarras de richesse*. Where to focus?10

The problems encountered by the dissipative adaptation theory--of which I have provided here only the most general sketch--are accompanied by yet another set of questions. To what extent is England's new theory at odds with currently accepted scientific paradigms? I will give only two examples of such a possible conflict. The first involves the distinction between the living and the nonliving. The second involves the question as to whether, or to what extent England's views are in contradiction with Darwinism.

First, the question of life and nonlife. We have a strong tendency in our thinking to disjoin life from nonlife. A quartz crystal is not alive. It is "dead." A mockingbird, by contrast, is the opposite: it is alive, and in no sense dead. And between the two we tend to think, there are no graduations. Life is life. Nonlife is nonlife. If this is our tendency, toward simple dualism, the theory of dissipative adaptation is its denial. Between nonliving and living phenomena on this theory, there are any number of intermediate phenomena which are

---

9 Brian Miller and Jeremy English, "Hot Wired," *Inference: International Review of Science* (May 24, 2020). Website: https://inference.review.com/article/hot-wired. Accessed 18 Feb 2022.

10 Gili Bisker and Jeremy England, "Nonequilibrium Associative Retrieval of Multiple Stored Self-Assembly Targets," *Proceedings of the National Academy of the Sciences* 115, no. 45 (8 November 2018): E1053-E1058. Also, Sumantra Sarker and Jeremy England, "Design of Conditions for Self-replication," *Physical Review E* 100, no. 2 (August 2019).

lifelike, though we cannot say they are living. One thinks for example of the BZ reaction and similar chemical reactions, which maintain the dynamism and cooperative unity of life. But as England correctly states, life is a package deal. Unless a system can reproduce and unless it exists in tandem with a cell membrane or something like it, we cannot say it is living. The most we can say is that it has some characteristics of the living. But if this is true, then much of nature is lifelike. Much more than we would have guessed.

The question of the distance between dissipative adaptation theory and Darwin's theory of evolution promises to be much debated and much discussed. One of the attractive features of Darwinism is its simplicity. It rests on two assumptions which seem quite clear: 1. genetic variation and 2. natural selection. The first of these Darwin understood as involving a series of minor changes to the genetic material ("point" mutations) taking place slowly over great lengths of time. The second consisted simply of the killing off of the "unfit" those species unable to compete in the struggle for existence. It is arguable that dissipative adaption theory casts doubt on, or at least requires the serious reformulation of, all three Darwinian assumptions. Genetic variation may well be not point-like but may involve systematic far-reaching transformations of the genes. Natural selection might turn out to be not so much a struggle for survival in a context of scarce resources as a being resolved by the creation of new dissipative forms. Emphasis on struggle and competition could be sidelined in favor of models stressing not warfare but cooperation.

None of this is resolved. Allison Eck speculates that on the terms of England's theory:

> Darwinian natural selection could be recast as a special case of the more generalized phenomenon of dissipative adaptation.[11]

One finds England making remarks like the following. The chemical activity we find in nature, he states, can produce adaptations "that do not necessarily require a Darwinian mechanism."[12] We may be able, he suggests, to find self-organization "even in the absence of self-replication and natural selection."[13] Where we might end up in evolutionary theory is not now entirely clear. But the suggestion is that for the first time Darwin's theory could receive serious reformulation.

---

[11] HSL, 7.

[12] Natalie Elliot, "The Origin Story," *Aeon Newsletter* (8 September 2020). Website: https://aeon.co/essays/physics-and-information-theory-give. Accessed 21 Feb 2022.

[13] LF, 168.

B. Metaphysical "Forcing": *Élan vital* and the Reconfiguration of Matter

This section will attempt to show in what respects England's and Bergson's viewpoints are similar. To repeat: England is in no way influenced by Bergson or by process philosophy generally. If anything, he is influenced by the ideas of Ludwig Wittgenstein, with their emphasis on language. The lack of influence or common intellectual background between England and Bergson makes the similarities between their viewpoints all the more striking

To describe these points of convergence it will be necessary to start from an analysis of the creative "spark" through which Bergson hopes to explain life and biological evolution: the vital impetus or *élan vital*. It seems a perilous starting point. If one examines his philosophy in terms of biological time one is immediately on solid scientific ground. Biological time is a concept with which scientists are familiar and which can be applied throughout the living organism. But if one starts with *élan vital*, what has one got? Of all of Bergson's central concepts, it seems the least useful, the least capable of creating meaning. I will argue that, surprisingly, this is not so. The notion of a life force as a source of unpredictable spontaneity and the emergence of strikingly dynamic form, finds close parallels in England's discoveries. We can use England to understand Bergson.

The argument will be twofold. In the first part, it will be contended that the *élan vital* is not a transcendent force operating outside the physical world, but a principle closely bound to and active in its relations to matter. In practice, it would be hard to distinguish between the vital impetus and the behavior of matter itself. This is certainly true in the cases that England describes, in which atomic and chemical arrays undergo transformative, creative interactions. The second part of this section will portray the three central components of dissipative adaptations: forcing, resonant response, and subsequent chemical and atomic transformation. These will be seen to parallel the temporal order and structure of Bergsonian evolution: which consists of a vital "push" coming out of the past, an interaction with available matter in the present and a resulting emergence of novel, unpredictable form: the making an organ, an organism, a tissue.

The *élan vital* as Bergson describes it can be understood in terms of his temporal hierarchy. It will thus have a duration different from--more prolonged than--those lower in the hierarchy. It will also attempt to impose its rhythm on matter as on living things.[14] If matter were what Newton believed, a set of inert corpuscles, this action of "consciousness or supraconsciousness"[15] on physical

---

[14] CE, 83.

[15] CE, 167.

nature would be unintelligible. But if matter, as Bergson holds, is a complex of varied durations, this action begins to become intelligible. We have, in total contrast with Descartes' mind-matter dualism, an interaction between two sorts of reality with a dynamic character in common.

More can be said. In Bergson's hierarchy—on this point, similar to Aristotle's—the higher levels cannot exist and cannot function without the lower. We recall that in Bergson's psychology the mind cannot function independently of the human motor and nervous system. This is true in two ways. If our brain is damaged we may lose consciousness or the capacity to use language. That is, the relation of consciousness to the physical body may be negative--resulting in the lowering of consciousness in its own hierarchy. Positively the brain and nervous system, by making available to us a wide variety of behaviors, also make it possible for us to come up with novel behaviors and thus express ourselves freely. The relation of the higher levels to the lower is thus two-sided, both positive and negative: This same ambiguity is found in the relations between the vital impetus and life. On the negative side the relative inertness of matter, Bergson states, may impede evolution.[16] On the positive side it is matter which provides life with the materials without which it cannot fashion new dynamic structures. Without matter the force of life would be impotent. Bergson, reflecting on his cosmology, speculates that until matter had reached its present form, life could not take hold and begin its development.[17]

Bergson's language makes this clear. Not only is the vital impetus present wherever there is matter. This impetus is capable of being immanent in matter. Thus the vital impetus "passes through matter"[18] is "loaded with matter,"[19] introduces the largest amount of indeterminism possible into matter.[20] That is, on his terms, life and matter, always in contact, can mutually interact.

England's process of dissipative adaptation has three components:

1. Forcing, a powerful influx of energy impacting the chemical network from without.
2. Resonance, the response of the chemical network to its energy input, a response, which England points out, an increased capacity to absorb energy, hence increased production of entropy.

---

[16] CE, 64-65.

[17] CE, 164.

[18] CE, 157.

[19] CE, 165.

[20] CE, 160.

3. Creativity, the active reconfiguration of prior chemical and physical arrays into forms which, utilizing increasing amounts of energy, are quite different from those present at the beginning of the dissipative process.

The dissipative processes which lead to these new forms are not random. They proceed until they coalesce into a steady state, termed an "end point." Here they continue to cycle at high energy, persisting indefinitely in (able to survive in) their environment. This process is not, strictly speaking, the behavior of a living thing. But it is lifelike.

The same three closely analogous phases occur in Bergson's account of the impact of the vital energy on matter. First there is the influx of creative energy: as we have termed it: a "push" coming out of the past. Then there is the response of "inert" matter to the destabilizing influence of this push.[21] Third, there is a transformation of the state, the structure of matter through the convergence of two radically contrasting factors. The energy imposed on nonliving matter, to repeat the point, is not England's purely physical energy. But the results of its impact are the same: the emergence of novel chemical complexes, the transformation of matter. The *élan vital*, we discover, does exactly what England's dissipative processes do: reconfiguring matter to produce more unified, active forms.

There is a fundamental point here which must not be overlooked. For traditional physics and chemistry, it has been taken as obvious that all things and processes are reducible to and entirely dependent on the behavior of a multitude of independent deterministic factors. In principle, on this assumption all natural phenomena are predictable, and with precision. It is this assumption, however, that the work of Prigogine, followed by Crooks and England, has put in question. It must not be assumed that when England talks about entropy and physical and chemical activity he is proposing the traditional viewpoint. Rather, he is subverting it. His theory of dissipative adaptation rests, rather, on two untraditional assumptions. First, absolute determinism does not hold for the physics of chaos, for which "sensitive dependence on initial conditions" entails inescapable unpredictability. There may be deterministic phenomena. But these do not appear far from equilibrium. We can postulate them. But we cannot find them.

The second assumption is bound to the first. On the nonlinear approach, we are no longer dealing with discrete particles, but with processes as a whole. That is, while the traditional standpoint is an inescapably atomistic concept of reality, the new one, assumes the opposite: holism. When England describes

---

[21] CE, 127-128.

the chemicals in a dissipative process as "cooperative," this is what he means. Such molecules work as a whole. They lose their rugged individualism and assume a group identity.

This changes everything. For the first time, discoveries within science challenge assumptions that science had held from the beginning, from the seventeenth century until now. Real unpredictability, real spontaneity, real dynamic wholes, processes with inherent temporal form: these now can be treated as facts in the world, not the mere products of some philosopher's fancy. In turn, attempts by philosophers to develop and frame such ideas no longer seem as vain as they once did.

In Bergson's time little if anything was done with nonlinear equations and fractal geometry did not exist. He was thus limited to using imagery from ordinary experience to try to elicit in the mind of his readers the explosive character of evolution. The images he used (the thrusting of a hand into iron filings,[22] the cavalry charge,[23] the firework display,[24] waves,[25] the exploding cannon shells[26] have a certain literary expressiveness and are indeed suggestive. If he were here today, he would have had two further, extremely helpful factors which he would certainly have appropriated. The first is a series of very concrete examples drawn from the new science of thermodynamic chaos, providing graphic insights into what we can mean by novelty, spontaneity, and the sudden unexpectedness of new form. The second is the satisfaction of realizing that once again ideas of his which had seemed extravagant or even empty, have received their measure of empirical support.[27]

---

[22] CE, 61.

[23] CE, 173.

[24] CE, 157.

[25] CE, 172.

[26] CE, 181.

[27] That I am not alone in this opinion is gratifying. Cf. James Di Frisco, "*Élan vital* Revisited: Bergson and the Thermodynamic Paradigm," *The Southern Journal of Philosophy* 53, no. 1 (March 2015): 54-73. Also, Naoki Sato, "Scientific *Élan Vital*: Entropy Deficit as a Unified Concept of Driving Forces of Life in a Hierarchical Biosphere Driven by Photosynthesis," *Molecular Diversity Preservation International* 12, no.2 (February 2012): 233-251.

XVI.

Brief Concluding Remarks

This book's title, *Getting Bergson Straight*, is intended as blunt and to the point. It makes a single claim. Intuitions in Bergson's sense, even if they might initially appear strange, can form the basis of new sciences or the rejuvenation of old ones. Simple as that. The fact that he was able to engender successful researches in the sciences provides one justification for this claim, which also derives support from an attentive analysis of his theory of knowledge. If we accept this point of view, then the widespread picture of Bergson as both anti-intellectual and anti-scientific needs to be rethought. He did not with his trenchant criticisms attempt to undermine the sciences. He tried to provoke new scientific studies and new modes of analysis.

Attacks on received opinion are rarely received gratefully. Most often they are greeted with cold indifference or harsh counterattacks. In Bergson's case, this tendency was compounded by the appearances of his thought. How could a philosophy that champions personal intuition, freedom and spontaneity be one which at the same time seeks to enter fruitfully into scientific thought with its emphasis on analysis and precision? This essay makes a concerted attempt to show how such a combination of opposites is actually possible. Bergson--in contrast with much of twentieth-century philosophy--attempts to create a philosophy that can accommodate both. He insists on both conceptual imagination in its almost anarchic refusal to be expressed in any algorithm and the strict scientific and technological approach which, among other things, helps us to exist in the world. Surely there is room somewhere for a both-and philosophy.

It will help to make two more points here. The first concerns the relations between philosophy and the arts and with human values generally. The second, not often discussed in this work but always a concern there is the question of what philosophy is and what it might be doing.

In one respect, the present work, if it has attempted to clear away conceptual confusions which stand in the way of making sense of Bergson, achieves a one-sided result. We have shown points at which the French philosopher was able to suggest fruitful directions in scientific research. But there is another side of his thought which has been neglected here. Bergson, the scientifically minded philosopher was also and at the same time an agent provocateur who overturned aesthetic dogmas and engendered new approaches in the arts. Bergson's situation certainly had a lot to do with his influence on the world of artists and critics.

Turn of the century Paris was the acknowledged world center of the arts, while Bergson's philosophy of intuition reigned there as the most celebrated approach to a vital reality. His influence on writers, painters and sculptors was omnipresent, both as a specific, particular influence and through the Zeitgeist which he had helped to transform. But that such a thinker could at the same time have posed serious challenges to both the artistic and to the scientific point of view seemed unlikely then--not conceivable. But it is conceivable, as we have seen. But the focus of this book, regrettably, has left his aesthetic influence to one side. The writer regrets this and invites others to redress the disbalance.

The second point, which concerns the function of philosophy, needs to be developed at greater length. It expresses both a regret for one-sidedness and a suggestion of possibilities. It will end with a reflection on the wrongheadedness of bottom-line mentalities, in philosophy especially.

There is no reason to limit the applicability of Bergson's insights to the sciences and the arts. There are many other possibilities. Failure to suggest some contrasting examples would be to commit the sin of one-sidedness. It would be to engage myopia. What follows is an enumeration of several efforts to apply his insights to several fields. The list, as should be obvious, is incomplete: 1. efforts by earlier 20th century biologists to apply Bergson's ideas to their fields[1] 2. the attempt to use his ideas to reformulate the modern concept of history[2] 3. rethinking our concepts of race and European colonialism[3] 4. efforts to reconceive modern visual culture[4] 5. an examination of the extent that Bergson's philosophy formed the basis of the political and literary negritude movement in the 1920's[5] 6. attempts to bring Bergson's philosophy in contact - productive contact-with the cognitive sciences[6] 7. applications of Bergsonism

---

[1] Emily Hering, "Henri Bergson's Creative Evolution and 20th Century British Biology," PhD Thesis, Leeds University, May 2020.

[2] Ter Schure, *Bergson and History: Transforming the Modern Regime of Historicity* (Albany: SUNY Press, 2019).

[3] Andrea Pitts and Mark William Westmoreland, *Beyond Bergson: Examining Race and Colonialism Through the Writings of Henri Bergson* (Albany: SUNY Press, 2019). Also, Souleymane Bachir Dagne, *Postcolonial Bergson* (New York: Fordham University Press, 2019), 144.

[4] Paul Atkinson, *Henri Bergson and Visual Culture: A Philosophy for a New Aesthetic* (New York: Bloomsbury / J.B. Taurus, 2019), 245.

[5] Donna V. Jones, *Racial Discourse of Life Philosophy* (New York: Columbia University Press, 2011), 240.

[6] Tim Moore, "Bergson and the Cognitive Sciences," 1996 (Revised 2013, 2017).

to the problems of city planning[7] 8. the effort to bring Bergson's philosophy into creative contact, with and to revivify, modern social philosophy and, above all, its concept of value.[8]

Finally, the author, if he has insisted that philosophy can be both conceptually fruitful and practical, by no means thinks it should be limited to the famous "bottom line." A thing, Aristotle once said, can be both good in itself and good for what it does. The pursuit of knowledge, the search for truth per se, is for this writer as they were for Bergson, valid in themselves. But there is no reason to keep the philosopher hemmed in. Plato was right to insist that the philosopher should be interrupted in his or her viewing of the forms and forced back into the cave, in an attempt to foster enlightenment there. Bergson goes farther than Plato. For him, a powerful new insight quite naturally seeks expression: both expression in the abstract and application to the world.

---

[7] Charissa N. Terranova, "Marcel Poete's Bergsonian Urbanism," *Journal of Urban History* 34, no. 6 (October 2020), 919-943; Benjamin Fraser, "Toward a Philosophy of the Urban: Henri Lefebvre's Uncomfortable Application of Bergsonism," *Environmental and Planning D: Society and Space* 26, no. 2 (April 2008): 338-358.

[8] Alexandre Lefebvre, *Human Rights as a Way of Life: On Bergson's Political Philosophy*, (Stanford: Stanford University Press, 2013); Alexandre Lefebvre and Melanie White, *Bergson, Politics and Religion* (Durham, NC; Duke University Press, 2015); Alexandre Lefebvre and Nils F. Schott, *Interpreting Bergson: Critical Essays* (New York: Cambridge University Press, 2020).

Bibliography

Adams, Richard P. "The Apprenticeship of William Faulkner." In *Tulane Studies in English*, Vol. 12, 1962, 113-155.

Aller, D.F. and Postel, J. "Eugeniusz Minkowski ou une vision de la schizophrénie." *L'évolution psychiatrique* 60, no. 4 (1995): 961-196.

Anderson, Scott. "The Psychobiotic Revolution." *New Scientist*, 243, no. 3246 (September 7, 2019): 24-28.

Anonymous. "List of Fractals by Hausdorff Dimension." Wikivisually. Website: http://wikivisually.com/wiki/List_of_fractals_by_Hausdorff_dimension. Accessed 20 Dec 2021.

Anonymous. "Obituary: Georges Lanteri-Laura." *History of Psychiatry*, 16, no. 3 (2005): 365-372.

Anonymous. "Our Memories are Packed with Thousands of Mugshots," *New Scientist* 240, no. 3200 (October 20, 2018): 17. DOI: 10.1016/S0262-4079(18)31 926-2

Anonymous. "The Grand Memory Illusion," *New Scientist* 240, no. 3201 (October 27, 2018): 31–32.

Anonymous. "What is Memory For?" *New Scientist* 240, no. 3201 (27 October 2018): 32-33.

Anonymous. *Bulletin de la société française de philosophie*, 22, no. 3 (1922): 102-113. In *Bergson and the Evolution of Physics*, edited by and translated by Pete A.Y. Gunter, 123-135. Knoxville: University of Tennessee Press, 1969.

L'Annunziale, Michael. *Radioactivity: Introduction and history*. New York: Elsevier, 2007.

Atkinson, Paul. *Henri Bergson and Visual Culture: A Philosophy for a New Aesthetic*. Bloomsbury (J.B. Taurus), 2019.

Bachelard, Gaston. "Noumène et microphysique." *Recherches Philosophiques* 1 (1932): 55-65.

Bailey H., K. Borer, F. Combley, H. Drumm, F. Krienen, F. Lange, E. Picasso, et al. "Relativistic Time Dilation for Positive and Negative Muons in a Circular Orbit." *Nature* 268, no. 5516 (1977): 301-35.

Balestra, Dominic J. "The Mind of Jean Piaget: Its Philosophical Roots." *Thought* 55, no. 210 (1988): 412-427.

Ball, Philip. "Reality in the Making." *New Scientist* 245, no. 3275 (2020): 35-38.

Benrubi, Isaac. *Souvenirs sur Henri Bergson*. Paris: Delachaux et Niestlé, 1942.

Bergson, Henri. "Bergson à Milič Čapek. July 3, 1938." In *Correspondances*, edited by André Robinet. Paris: Presses Universitaires de France, 2002.

_____. *Creative Evolution*, translated by A. Mitchell. London: Palgrave Macmillan, 2007.

_____. *The Creative Mind*, translated by M. Andison. New York: The Philosophical Library, 1946.

_____. *Duration and Simultaneity*. 2nd Ed., translated by Leon Jacobson. New York: Bobbs-Merrill Company, 1965.

_____. *La pensée et le mouvant*. Paris: Presses Universitaires de France, 2014.

_____. *Matter and Memory*, translated by N. M Paul and W. S. Palmer. New York: Zone Books, 2005.

_____. *Time and Free Will*, translated by F. L. Pogson. London: George Allen & Ltd, 1950.

Berrios, G.E. *History of Mental Symptoms: Descriptive Psychopathology Since the Nineteenth Century*. Cambridge: Cambridge University Press, 1996.

Bisker, Gili and Jeremy England. "Nonequilibrium Associative Retrieval of Multiple Stored Self-Assembly Targets." *Proceedings of the National Academy of the Sciences* 115, no. 45 (November 8, 2018): E1053-E1058.

Blondel, Charles. "Insane Thought and Language." *The Troubled Conscience and the Insane Mind*, translated by F.G. Crookshank. London: Kegan Paul Trench Trubrer & Co. 1928, 68-91. (Reprint: Routledge, 2014.)

_____. *La Conscience Morbide: Essai de Psychopathologie Générale*. Paris: Felix Alcan, 1914. (Republished by Wentworth Press, an imprint of Creative Media Partners.)

Bouligand, Y. and Chanu, J. "Introducion biologique à la notion de structure dissipative." In *La Morphogenèse de la Biologie aux Mathématiques*, edited by Y. Bouligand. Paris: Maloine, 1980.

Boutroux, Émile. *The Contingency of the Laws of Nature*. Translated by F. Rothwell. Chicago: Open Court, 1916, 196. Cf. *De la contingence des lois de la nature*. Paris: Librairie Germer Bailler, 1874. Bergson may also have been referring to the similar views of Charles Sanders Peirce.

Brainard, J., ed. "Cosmic Law Renamed to Expand Credit." *Science* 362, no. 6414 (2018): 504.

Brillouin, Léon. *Science and Information Theory*. 2nd Ed. New York: Dover Edition, 2013.

de Broglie, Louis. "The Concepts of Contemporary Physics and Bergson's Ideas on Time and Motion." In *Bergson and the Evolution of Physics*, edited and translated by Pete A.Y. Gunter. Knoxville: University of Tennessee Press, 1969, 45-62. (De Broglie's essay was first published in his *Physique et microphysique*, 1947.)

Brumbaugh, Robert S. and Nathaniel M. Lawrence. *Philosophical Themes in Modern Education*. Boston: Haughton Mifflin, 1973.

Buzsaki, Gyorgy. *Rhythms of the Brain*. Oxford: Oxford University Press, 2006.

Canales, Jimena. "Dead and Alive: Micro-cinematography Between Physics and Biology." *Configurations* 23, no. 2 (2015): 235-251.

_____. *The Physicist and the Philosopher: Einstein, Bergson, and the Debate that Changed Our Understanding of Time*. Princeton: Princeton University Press, 2015.

Čapek, Milič. *Bergson and Modern Physics*. Dordrecht-Holland: D. Reidel, 1971.

_____. "The Philosophical Significance of Piaget's Researchers on the Genesis of the Concpet of Time." In *Naturalistic Epistemology*, edited by A. Shimony and D. Nails. Boson: D. Reidel, 1987, 91-118.

Carrel, Alexis. *Man, the Unknown.* New York: Harper and Row, 1935.

_____. "The New Cytology." *Science* 73, no. 1890 (March 20, 1931): 297-303.

de Chardin, Pierre Teilhard. Introduction to *The Phenomenon of Man.* Written by Julian Huxley. New York: Harper and Row, 1961.

Chevalier, Jacques. *Entretiens avec Bergson.* Paris: Plon, 1949.

Clegg, Brian. "The Origin of Life: A New Theory Suggests Physics has the Answer." *BBC Focus Magazine* 322 (October 25, 2019).

Corsini, Raymond and Danny Wedding, eds. *Current Psychotherapies.* 7th Ed. New York: Thompson, 2005.

de Coster, Sylvain. "In Memoriam La psychologie sociologique de Charles Blondel." *Revue Internationale de Psychologie* 1, no. 3 (1939): 578-581.

Crooks, Gavin. "Entropy Production Fluctuation and the Nonequilibrium Work Relation for Free Energy Differences." *Physical Review E* G0 (1999): 2721.

Dagne, Souleymane Bachir. *Postcolonial Bergson.* New York: Fordham University Press, 2019.

Deleuze, Gilles. *Bergsonism,* translated by H. Tomlinson and B. Haberjam. New York: Zone Books, 1991.

Di Frisco, James. "Élan vital Revisited: Bergson and the Thermodynamic Paradigm." *The Southern Journal of Philosophy* 53, no. 1 (March 2015): 54-73.

Dingle, Herbert. Introduction to *Duration and Simultaneity.* 2nd Ed. Written by Henri Bergson, edited and translated by Leon Jacobson. New York: Bobbs-Merrill Company, 1965, i-xlii.

Duhring, Elie. *Einstein et Bergson: La querelle du temps.* Paris: Presses Universitaires de France, 2020.

_____. "Temps réel, temps universal, temps cosmologique: Trois dimensions de la cosmologie Bergsonienne." *Tout ouverte,* edited by Shin Abiko, Hisashi Fujita, and Masato Goda. New York: Olms, 2015.

Dwelshauvers, Georges. *Traité de psychologie.* Paris: Payot, 1934.

Early, Joseph E. "Self-Organization and Agency: In Chemistry and in Process Philosophy." *Process Studies* 11, no. 4 (1981): 242-258.

Ebbinghaus, H. *Über das Gedächtnis.* Leipzig: Duncker und Humblot, 1005.

Eck, Allison. "How do You Say 'Life' in Physics? A New Theory Which Sheds Light on the Emergence of Life's Complexity." *Nautilus* (July 10, 2017). Website: https://nautil.us/issue/50/emergence/how-do-you-say-life-in-physics-rp. Accessed 20 Dec 2021. (This article was originally published in *Adaptation,* March 2016.)

Edlund, Matthew. *Psychological Time and Mental Illness.* New York: Gardner Press, Inc., 1987.

Einstein, Albert. *The Meaning of Relativity.* Princeton, NJ: Princeton University Press, 1974.

_____. *Relativity: The Special and the General Theory,* translated by W. Lawson. London: Methuen, 1962.

Ellenberger, Henri. *The Discovery of the Unconscious.* New York: Basic Books, 1970.

Elliot, Natalie. "The Origin Story." *Aeon Newsletter,* September 8, 2020. Website: https://aeon.co/essays/physics-and-information-theory-give. Accessed 21 Sep 2021.

Elwes, Richard. *Mathematics Without the Boring Bits.* New York: Metro Books, 2011.

England, Jeremy. *Every Life is on Fire: How Thermodynamics Explains the Origins of Living Things.* New York: Basic Books, 2020.

England, Jeremy. "Statistical Physics of Self Replication." *Journal of Chemical Physics* 139, no. 121923 (August 2013).

Euler, Leonard. *Theoria motus corporum solidurum seu rigidorum.* (Rostochii et Gryphiswaldiae: Litteris et impensis A.F. Rose, 1765). Website: https:// ecommons. cornell.edu/handle/1813/57675 Accessed 10 Feb 2022.

Falconer, Kenneth. *Fractals: A Very Short Introduction.* Oxford: Oxford University Press, 2013.

Fedi, Laurent. "Un cas de réception: Piaget lecture de *L'évolution créatice.*" In *Les Annales Bergsoniennes* IV. Paris: Presses Universitaires de France, 2008, 237-254.

Finnbogason, Guðmundur. *L'Intelligence sympathique,* translated by André Courmont. Paris: Felix Alcan, 1913. (Bibliothèque de philosophie contemporaine.)

Foster, D.G. "Are We Trying to Banish Biological Time?" *Cerebrum. Dana Foundation* (April 1, 2004). Website: https://www.dana.org/article/are-we-trying-to-banish-biological-time/. Accessed 09 Jan 2022.

Foster, Russell G. and Leon Kreitzman. *Rhythms of Life.* New Haven: Yale University Press, 2005.

Frankel, Miriam. "Clock Watchers." *The New Scientist* 253, no. 3367 (January 1, 2022): 46-49.

Fraser, Benjamin. "Toward a Philosophy of the Urban: Henri Lefebvre's Uncomfortable Application of Bergsonism" *Sage Journals Environmental and Planning D: Society and Space* 26, no. 2 (April 2008): 338-358.

Freud, Sigmund. "Letter to James Jackson Putnam, July 8, 1915." In *James Jackson Putnam and Psychoanalysis,* 188-191, edited by Nathan G. Hale, Jr., and translated by J. B. Heller. Cambridge, MA: Harvard Univ Press, 1971.

_____. *The Life and Works of Sigmund Freud,* 3 Volumes, edited by Ernst Jones. New York: Basic Books, 1953-1958.

Friedman, David M. *The Immortalists: Charles Lindbergh, Dr. Alexis Carrel, and Their Daring Quest to Live Forever.* New York: Harper Collins, 2008.

Frisch, D.H. and J.H Smith, J.H. "Measurement of the Relativistic Time Dilation using M-Mesons." *American Journal of Physics* 31, no. 5 (1963): 342-355.

Fuentenebra, F., and G.E Berrios. "Charles Blondel and *La Conscience Morbide.*" In *History of Psychiatry,* Vol. VIII, 1997.

Golombek, Diego A., Ivana L. Bussi, and Patricia V. Agostino. "Minutes, Days and Years: Molecular Interactions Among Different Scales of Biological Timing." *Philosophical Transactions: Biological Sciences* 369, no. 1637 (March 5, 2014): 1-12.

Goodwin, Donald W. "Alcoholism and Genetics, The Sins of the Fathers." *Archives of General Psychiatry* 42, no. 2 (1985): 171-174.

Grossman, Morris. "A Glimpse at Some Unpublished Santayana Manuscripts." *Journal of Philosophy* 61, no. 1 (1964): 61-69.

Gunter, Pete A.Y. *Bergson and the Evolution of Physics.* Knoxville: University of Tennessee Press, 1969.

Gunter, Pete A. Y. "Bergson and Jung." *Journal of the History of Ideas* 43, no. 4 (1982): 635-652.

_____. "Bergson and Non-Linear Non-Equilibrium Thermodynamics: An Application Method." *Revue Internationale de Philosophie* 2, no. 177 (1991): 108-121.

_____. "Bergson and Proust: A Question of Influence." In *Understanding Bergson, Understanding Modernism*, 157-176. New York: Bloomsbury, 2013.

_____. "Bergson, Materialization and the Peculiar Nature of Space." *Lo Sguardo* 1, no. 26 (2018): 231-245.

_____. "Bergson's Creation of the Possible." *SubStance* 114, no. 36 (2007): 1-9.

_____. "Bergson's Divided Line and Minkowski's Psychiatry: The Way Down." In *Chromatikon IV*, 107-119. Louvain: Presses Universitaires de Louvain, 2008.

_____. "Bergson's Theory of Matter and Modern Cosmology." *Journal of the History of Ideas* 32, no. 4 (1971): 525-543.

_____. *Henri Bergson: A Bibliography*. 2nd ed. Bowling Green, OH: Philosophy Documentation Center, 1986.

_____. "The Heuristic Force of Creative Evolution." *Southwestern Journal of Philosophy* 1, no. 3 (1970): 111-118.

_____. "A Tale of Two Memories. Bergson and the Creation of Memory Science." *Memory & Matter* 11, no. 2 (2013): 137-152.

Hafele, J.C. and R.E Keating. "Around the World Atomic Clocks Predicted Relativistic Time Gains." *Science* 177, no. 4044 (1972): 166-168.

Hamilton, David. *The First Transplant Surgeon: The Flawed Genius of Alexis Carrel*. New York: World Scientific, 2016.

Hayflick, L. "How and Why We Age." *Experimental Gerontology* 33, no. 7-8 (1996): 639-653.

Hering, Emily. "Henri Bergson's *Creative Evolution* and 20th-Century British Biology." PhD Thesis. University of Leeds, May 2020.

Herubel, Marcel. "Review of *L'évolution créatrice* by Henri Bergson," *L'année biologique* 15 (1910): 532-35.

Hinkle, Beatrice. "Jung's Libido Theory and the Bergsonian Philosophy." *New York Medical Journal* 30 (1914): 1080-1086.

_____. *Recreating the Individual: Study of Psychological Types and Their Relation to Psychoanalysis*. London: George Allen & Unwin, 1923.

Huang, R. C. "The Discovery of Molecular Mechanisms for Circadian Rhythms." *Biomedical Journal* 41, no. 1 (2018): 5-8.

Infeld, Leopold. *Albert Einstein*. Revised Ed. New York: Charles Scribner's Sons, 1950.

Iselin, H. K. *Zur Entsehung von C. G. Jungs "Psychologische Typen": Die Briefwchsel zwischen C. G. Jung und Hans Schmidt-Guisan im Lichte ihrer Freundshaft*. Aarou: Saverlander, 1982.

Jones, Donna V. *Racial Discourse of Life Philosophy*. New York: Columbia University Press, 2011.

Jones, Ernest. *The Formative Years and the Great Discoveries, 1856-1900*, Vol 1. In *The Life and Work of Sigmund Freud*. New York: Basic Books, 1953.

_____. *Years of Maturity, 1901-1919*, Vol 2. In *The Life and Work of Sigmund Freud*. New York: Basic Books, 1956.

_____. *The Last Phase, 1920-1939*, Vol 3. In *The Life and Work of Sigmund Freud*. New York: Basic Books, 1958.

Jung, Carl Gustav. *C. G. Jung Speaking: Interviews and Encounters*, edited by W. McGuire and R.F.C. Hull. Princeton, NJ: Princeton University Press, 1977.

_____. *Collected Papers in Analytical Psychology*, Translated by M. D. Elder, and edited by C.E. Long. London: 1922.

_____. "The Content of the Psychoses, Part II, 1914." In *Collected Papers*, 351.

_____. "Instinct and the Unconscious." In *Collected Papers*, 247.

_____. "On Some Crucial Points in Psychoanalysis." In *Collected Papers*, 274-275.

_____. *Psychological Types*. Princeton: Princeton University Press, 1971, 608.

Kern, Stephen. "Time and Medicine." *Annals of Internal Medicine* 132, no. 1 (2000): 3-8.

Kumar, Shiv. *Bergson and the Stream of Consciousness Novel*. London: Blackie, 1962.

_____. *Virginian Woolf and Bergson's 'Durée.'* Hoshiarpur, India: Vishveshvaranand Book Agency, 1957.

Lahav, Noam. *Biogenesis: Theories of Life's Origin*. New York: Oxford University Press, 1998.

Laing, Ronald D. "Minkowski and Schizophrenia." *Review of Existential Psychology* 9 (1963): 195-207.

Landecker, Hannah. "Cellular Features: Microcinematography and Film Theory." *Critical Enquiry* 31, no. 4 (2006).

Langsdorf, Lenore. "Schutz's Bergsonian Analysis of the Structure of Consciousness." *Human Studies* 8, no. 4 (1985): 316-324.

Laughlin, Robert B. *A Different Universe: Reinventing Physics from the Bottom Down*. New York: Basic Books, 2005.

Lecomte du Noüy, Mary. *The Road to Human Destiny*. New York: Longmans, Green, and Co., 1955.

Lecomte du Noüy, Pierre. *Le temps et la vie*. Paris: Gallimard, 1936.

_____. "Recherches éxper. et applie. des méthodes de la mesure et de calcul à un phénomène biologique: la cicatrisation." Thèse Ac. Sc. Paris, Dec 18, 1947. Printed Paris: Gauthier Villars.

Lefebvre, Alexandre, and Nils F. Schott. *Interpreting Bergson: Critical Essays*. Cambridge. Cambridge University Press, 2020.

Lefebvre, Alexandre. *Human Rights as a Way of Life: On Bergson's Political Philosophy*. Stanford: Stanford University Press, 2013.

Lefebvre, Alexandre, and Melanie White. *Bergson, Politics and Religion*, Durham, NC; Duke University Press, 2015.

Lovejoy, A.O. *Bergson and Romantic Evolutionism*. Berkeley: University of California Press, 1914.

_____. *The Reason the Understanding and Time*. Baltimore: The Johns Hopkins Press, 1961.

Lowrie, G.M. "The Scientific Contributions of Alexis Carrel." *Clinical Cardiology* 10, no.7 (1987): 428-430.

Lydie, Adolphe. *La dialectique des images chez Bergson.* Paris: Presses Universitaires de France, 1951.

Mandelbrot, Benoit. "How Long is the Coast of Britain?" *Science* 156, no. 3775 (1967): 636-638.

Mandelbrot, Benoit. *The Fractal Geometry of Nature.* New York: W. H. Freeman and Company, 1983.

Maxwell, James Clerk. "On Action at a Distance." In *The Scientific Papers of James Clerk-Maxwell,* Vol. LIV, 311-323. Cambridge: Cambridge University Press, 2013.

Maxwell, James Clerk. *A Treatise on Electricity and Magnetism.* Oxford: Clarendon Press, 1875.

May, Rollo. *The Discovery of Being: Writings in Existential Psychology.* New York: W.W. Norton and Company, 1983.

McDougall, William and Mary Smith. "Some Experiments in Learning and Attention." *British Journal of Psychology* 10, no. 2-3(1919-1920): 199-209.

Medica. "Biological Clock and Drug Addiction." *MEDICA Magazine,* 2019. Website: https://www.medica-tradefair.com/en/News/Archive/Biological_Clock_and_Drug_Addiction. Accessed 20 Dec 2021.

Miller, Brian and Jeremy England. "Hot Wired." *Inference: International Review of Science* (May 24, 2020). Website: https://inference.review.com/article/hot-wired. Accessed 18 Feb 2022.

Minkowski, Eugene. *Au-delà du rationalisme morbide.* Paris: Ed. L'Harmattan, 1997.

_____. *Lived Time,* translated by Nancy Metzel. Evanston, IL: Northwestern University Press, 1970.

_____. *Traité de psychopathologie.* Paris: Institut Synthelabo, 1999.

Moore, Tim. "Bergson and the Cognitive Sciences," 1996 (Revised 2013, 2017).

Mourgue, Raoul. *Neurobiologie de l'hallucination. Essai d'une variété particulière de désintégration de la fonction.* Pref. H. Bergson. Brussels: Maurice Lamerton, 1932.

Mourgue, Raoul, and Constantin von Monakow. *Introduction biologique a l'étude de la Neurologie et de la Psychopathologie.* Paris: Alcan, 1928.

Newton, Isaac. *Principia, Vol. 1: The Motions of Bodies.* Berkeley: University of California Press, 1962.

Parnas, Josef. "Introduction to History and Epistemology of Psychopathology." In *Philosophical Issues in Psychiatry,* 28, edited by K. S. Kendler and J. Parnas. Oxford: Oxford University Press, 2015.

Peirce, Charles S. "The Doctrine of Necessity Examined." *Monist* 2, no. 3 (1892): 321-337.

Piaget, Jean. "Autobiographical note." In *A History of Psychology in Autobiography,* edited by E. Boring et al. New York: Russell and Russell, 1952, 237-256.

Pilard, Nathalie. *Jung and Intuition.* London: Karnac, 2015.

Pind, J. L. "Guðmundur, Finnbogason: 'Sympathetic Understanding' and early Icelandic Psychology." *History of Psychology,* 11(2), 2008, 75-100.

Pitts, Andrea and Mark William Westmoreland. *Beyond Bergson: Examining Race and Colonialism Through the Writings of Henri Bergson.* Albany: SUNY, 2019.

Prigogine, Ilya. *From Being to Becoming.* San Francisco: W.H. Freeman, 1980.

Prigogine, Ilya, and I. Stenger. *Order Out of Chaos*. New York: Bantam, 1984.

Proust, Marcel. *À la recherche du temps perdu*. Paris: Gallimard, 1946-47 (in 15 volumes).

Przemslau, Prusinkewics and Aristid Lindenmayer. *The Algorithimic Beauty of Plants*. New York: Springer-Verlag, 1990.

Reichenbach, Hans. *The Direction of Time*, edited by Maria Reichenbach. Chicago: University of Chicago Press, 1971.

Reuillard, Gabrielle. in *Les Hommes du jour*. (Article quoted at length in *Current Opinion*, LVI, May 1914.)

Reznikov, N., M. Bilton, L. Lari, M.M. Stevens, and R. Kroger. "Fractal-like Hierarchical Organization of Bone Begins at the Nanoscale." *Science* 360, no. 6388 (2018): 507.

Roustan, Désiré. *Psychologie*. Paris: Delagrave, 1911.

Russell, Bertrand. *The ABC of Relativity*. London: Allen and Unwin, 1962.

_____. *Mysticism and Logic and Other Essays*. London: Allen & Unwin, 1910.

_____. *Our Knowledge of the External World*. Coppell, Tx: Didactic Press, 2017.

_____. *The Philosophy of Bergson, With a Reply by H. Wildon Carr and a Rejoinder by Bertrand Russell*. Cambridge: Bowes and Bowes, 1914.

Santayana, Georges. *Winds of Doctrine: Studies in Contemporary Opinion*. Kassel, Germany: Parthenon Books, 2016. (Originally published 1913.)

Sarker, Sumantra, and Jeremy England. "Design of Conditions for Self-replication." *Physical Review E* 100, no. 2 (August 2019).

Sass, Louis A. "Self and World in Schizophrenia." *Philosophy, Psychiatry, and Psychology* 8, no.4 (2001): 258.

Sato, Naoki. "Scientific Élan Vital: Entropy Deficit as a Unified Concept of Driving Forces of Life in a Hierarchical Biosphere Driven by Photosynthesis." *Molecular Diversity Preservation International* 12, no. 2 (2012): 233-251.

Schachter, Daniel. *Searching for Memory*. New York: Basic Books, 1996.

Scheler, Max. *The Nature of Sympathy*, translated by P. Heath. London: Routledge and Kegan Paul, 1954.

Schrecker, Paul. "Individual Psychological Significance of First Childhood Recollections." *Journal of Individual Psychology* 29, no. 2 (1973): 146-156.

Schrödinger, Erwin. "The Present Situation in Quantum Mechanics. A Translation of Schrödinger's 'Cat Paradox'," translated by J. D. Trimmer. *Proceedings of the American Philosophical Society* 121, no. 5 (1981): 323-338.

Schure, Ter. *Bergson and History: Transforming the Modern Regime of Historicity*. Albany: SUNY Press, 2019.

Schutz, Alfred. *Life Forms and Meaning Structure*. New York: Routledge, 2014.

Schwalm, Dirk, et al., "Test of Time Dilation Using Stored Li+ Ions as Clocks at Relativistic Speeds." *Physical Review Letters* 113 (September 4, 2014).

Sherry, Jay. "Beatrice Hinkle and the Early History of Jungian Psychology in New York." *Behavioral Science* 2, no. 3 (2013): 492-500.

Sinclair, Mark. *Bergson*. London: Routledge, 2019.

Smolin, Lee. *Einstein's Unfinished Revolution*. New York: Penguin Press, 2019.

Sorel, Georges. *Reflections on Violence*, edited by J. Jennings. Cambridge: Cambridge University Press, 1999.

Sorel, Georges. *The Illusions of Progress*. Berkeley: University of California Press, 1969.

Spaier, Albert. *La pensée concrète*. Paris: Alcan, 1927.

Spanegal, Rainer, Alan Rosenwasser, Gunter Schumann, and Dipak Sarkar. "Alcohol Consumption and the Body's Biological Clock." *Alcohol Clinical and Experimental Research* 29, no.8 (2005): 1550-1557.

Strammer, Bryan M., and Graham A. Dunn. "Cells on Film: The Past and Future of Cinemicroscopy." *Journal of Cell Science* 128, no. 1 (2015): 9-13.

Szasz, George. "It's Time for Chronomedicine." *British Columbia Medical Journal* (27 June 2019). Website: http://www.bcmj.org/blog/it-s-timechronomedicine. Accessed 10 Jan 2022.

Terranova, Charissa N. "Marcel Poete's Bergsonian Urbanism." *Journal of Urban History* 34, no. 6 (October 2020): 919-943.

Thaiss, Christopher A., Maayan Levy, and Eran Elinay. "Chronobiomics: The Biological Clock as a New Principle in Host-Microbial Interactions." *PLoS Pathog* 11, no. 10 (8 October 2015): e1005113.

_____. "Disrupting Gut Bacteria Circadian Rhythm Leads to Serious Health Consequences." *Chronobiology: Timing is Everything.* 15 Aug 2018. Website: https://www.chronobiology.com/?s=Disrupting+Gut+Bacteria+Circadian+Rhythm+Leads+to+Serious+Health+Consequences. Accessed 20Dec2021.

Torres, Nuno. "Intuition and Ultimate Reality in Psychoanalysis: Bion's Implicit Use of Bergson's and Whitehead's Notions." In *Bion's Sources*, edited by N. Torres and R.D. Hinshelwood. New York: Routledge, 2013, 20-34.

Vandel, Albert. *L'homme et l'évolution*. 13th Ed. Paris: Gallimard, 1958.

Vidal, Fernando. "Jean Piaget's Early Critique of Mendelism: La notion de l'espèce suivant l'ecole mendélienne," *History and Philosophy of the Life Sciences* 14, no.1 (1992): 113-115.

Vidal, Fernando. "*La vanité de la nomenclature*: Un manuscrit inédit de Jean Piaget," *History and Philosophy of the Life Sciences* 6, no.1 (1984): 75-106.

Villagran, Jose M. "Consciousness Disorders in Schizophrenia: A Forgotten Land for Psychopathology," *International Journal of Psychology and Psychological Theory* 3, no. 2 (2003): 216

von Monakow, Constantin. *Emotions, Morality, and the Brain*. Washington: Nervous and Mental Disease Publishing, 1925.

Wagner, H. R. *A Bergsonian Bridge to Phenomenological Psychology*. Lanham, MD: University Press of America, 1984.

Wallon, Henri. "The Psychological and Sociological Study of the Child" in *The World of Henri Wallon*, translated by D. Nicholson Smith.

Wheeler, J.A and W.H. Zurek, eds. *Quantum Theory and Measurement*. Princeton: Princeton University Press, 1983.

Whitehead, Alfred North. *An Enquiry Concerning the Principle of Natural Knowledge*. 2nd Ed. Eastford, CT: Martino Fine Books, 2017.

_____. *Science and the Modern World*. New York: The Free Press, 1967

_____. *The Concept of Nature*. Cambridge: Cambridge University Press, 1955.

Williamson, Joel. *William Faulkner and Southern History*. New York: Oxford University Press, 1993.

Witkowski, J.A. "Alexis Carrel and the Mysticism of Tissue Culture." *Medical History* 23, no. 3 (1977): 279-296.

_____. "Dr. Carrel's Immortal Cells." *Medical History* 24, no. 2 (1980): 129-142.

Wittenstein, Kate. "The Feminist Uses of Psychoanalysis: Beatrice Hinkle and the Foreshadowing of Modern Feminism in the United States." *Journal of Women's History* 10, no. 2 (1998): 38-62.

Worms, Frederick and Philippe Soulez. *Bergson*. Paris: Flammarion, 1997.

Wyss, Dieter. *Psychoanalytic Schools from the Beginning to the Present*, translated by G. Onn. New York: Jason Aronson, Inc., 1973.

Index